Shepherding the Sheep in Smaller Churches

Paul W. Powell

ANNUITY BOARD

OF THE SOUTHERN
BAPTIST CONVENTION

Dedication

To the staff of the Member Services Division of the Annuity Board:

Senior Vice President:	Frank Schwall
Vice Presidents:	Curtis Crofton
	James Haynes
	Bob Henry
	Bruce Sides
	Brad Thompson
Managers:	Michael Bailey
	John Hancock
	Susan May
	Don McLeod
	Elías Pantoja
	Harry Russell
	Michael Sims
Account Specialists:	John Baergen
	Dixie Beard
	Cindy Rodden
	Donna Sharp
Personal Marketing:	Mike Ford
	Dick Richard
Secretarial Staff:	Rita Brewer
	Dyna Hasse
	Nora Mercado
	Dorothy Prange
	Judy Robinson
	Mary Stripling

Table of Contents

Introduction

Introduction

This book was written at the suggestion of the staff of the Member Services Division of the Annuity Board. Headed by Frank Schwall, they are daily among the churches and with pastors. They share their sorrows, feel their frustrations, and help them bear their burdens.

Like the apostle Paul, the "care of the churches" comes upon them daily. They share a special burden for our smaller churches and their ministers. That's why they said we needed this book.

It is not a book of theory. It is, rather, a book of a practical ideas drawn from my years in the trenches and from talking to hundreds of pastors who labor there daily.

It is written to encourage, to inspire, to motivate the big people who serve in little places. Little, of course, is a relative term. Christ loved the church and gave himself for it. If such a great price was paid for the church, no one has a right to call any church small. Some are simply not as large as others.

The smaller church is the backbone of the kingdom of God. By their sheer numbers alone they carry the work of God forward. As they go, so goes the kingdom.

According to the 1994 Annual Church Profile of Southern Baptist churches, there are 8,268 congregations with less than 100 members, and 8,849 more with memberships between 100 and 199. More than 58 percent of our churches have less than 300 total membership.

It is for them and their pastors I have written this little volume. If they find it helpful, it will have fulfilled my purpose in writing it.

— Paul Powell

Chapter 1

You and Your Church Can Make a Difference

Ours is a denomination of smaller churches. That's really who we are. Just look at the statistics. Of the 39,910 Southern Baptist Convention congregations, the average church has 260 resident members, averages 88 people in Sunday School attendance and their annual receipts are $145,709. According to statistics there are approximately 255,000 churches of all denominations in America. Of that number, 100,000 have fewer than 50 people in attendance.

Despite the fact that the number of mega-churches, congregations that average more than 2,000 worshippers each Sunday, has climbed from 10 in 1970 to more than 300 in all denominations today, the smaller church is still the backbone of the kingdom of God.

A Smaller Church Can Do a Big Work

But don't let the size of a church fool you. Many a smaller church has done a big work for God. It's not the size of a church that determines the size of its impact for the Lord. Let me cite two examples:

The first is Belfalls Baptist Church, Belfalls, Texas, where I began my ministry 40 years ago. Belfalls is a small farming community in central Texas, located 30 miles south of Waco. It gets its name because it is located on the county line between Bell and Falls county. It was once a thriving farming community, but through the years the young people grew up and moved away, their parents grew old, and the farms consolidated. A few years ago the little church closed its doors for the last time.

When I went to my first pastorate there in 1955, the community had a cotton gin, grocery store, blacksmith shop, beauty shop, tavern, and a Baptist church. In my year and a half as pastor, we averaged between 50 and 60 in Sunday School. The little church had an effective ministry of evangelism, worship, fellowship, missions support, as well as providing a preaching place for young Baylor ministerial students.

Through the years the church has had a significant ministry in that respect alone. In addition to producing outstanding pastors such as Brian Harbour, First Baptist Church, Richardson, Texas; and Jim Johnson, pastor of Second Ponce de Leon Church, Atlanta, Georgia; it helped train the presidents of three Southern Baptist institutions and agencies.

- Arthur Rutledge, the late executive of the Home Mission Board.
- Robert Sloan, president of Baylor University.
- I, Paul Powell, president of the Annuity Board.

Not bad for one smaller church, huh?

The second church is Pecan Grove Baptist Church near Gatesville, Texas, west of Waco. Located on the edge of the Texas ranch lands, it was the beginning place for the ministry of W. A. Criswell, pastor of First Baptist Church, Dallas, Texas, for 50 years; Baker James Cauthen, president of the Foreign Mission Board of the Southern Baptist Convention for a quarter century; and many outstanding pastors such as Ray Mayfield, Jr. and LeRay Fowler.

A significant contribution for one smaller church, wouldn't you say?

Each year Baylor University honors three churches of varying sizes for their contribution to the kingdom of God — a smaller church, a medium-sized church, and a large church. Recently, Pecan Grove Church was chosen as the smaller church to be honored. At Baylor's annual endowment banquet, where these churches were recognized, the chairman of the deacons was asked how he accounted for the fact that his church had produced so many outstanding pastors. The old rancher replied, "The way you put a saddle on a horse the first time usually determines the kind of horse it will be. At Pecan Grove we know how to put a saddle on 'em."

There are countless smaller churches all across America that don't have massive crowds, that don't have big buildings, and that don't have large budgets, but they give young preachers a good start in the ministry. They know how to "put a saddle on 'em." In addition, they provide a witness to the lost, a place to worship the Lord Sunday by Sunday, an opportunity for fellowship and ministry to the people of God in their area, and are a strong supporter of missions at home and abroad. And that's no small thing.

It's an Honor to Serve Anywhere

The important thing about a church is not the size of its building or the size of its membership, but the size of its vision. All of my life I've heard the saying, "It's not the size of the dog in the fight, but the size of the fight in the dog that matters." The same is true of churches.

So even a smaller church can do a big work for God if it really wants to. As Winfred Moore said, "There are no small churches except those made up of little people."

And, there is no small work for God, only small places to do it, so we ought to consider it an honor to serve anywhere in God's vineyard. The poet put it well when he wrote:

Master, where shall I work today?
And my love flowed warm and free.
He pointed out a tiny spot
And said, 'Tend that for me.'
But I answered him quickly
'Oh, no. Not there.
Not that little place for me.'
For not one could see
No matter how well my work was done.
Not that little place for me.
The word he spoke, it was not stern,
He answered me tenderly.
'Disciple, search that heart of thine.
Are you working for them or for me?'
Nazareth was just a little place
And so was Galilee.

Remember Your Priorities

How do you measure a church anyway? It is not, as we have been led to believe, by the number of people on its staff, the multiplication of worship services, the amount of its budget, the array of its programs to meet every emotional, recreational, and entertainment need of its membership, or even the gathering of a crowd.

Crowds can be gathered by less than noble means. Jesus refused to succumb to the temptation to gather a crowd and gain a following by using spectacular but unscriptural means during his temptation experience.

The measure of a church is in the fulfilling of its mission. Someone has said, "Success is just another form of failure if you forget what your priorities are." A church must not forget what its priorities are. If bringing in the masses means failure to address the deep spiritual needs of all the people, then the church cannot be deemed a success.

What is the mission of the church? Until we know what the church is to do, we cannot properly measure the success or failure, the greatness or smallness, of any one church. No church needs to sit around wondering why it is here or what it is to do. The scriptures tell us plainly that our mission is the same as the mission of Christ.

Jesus defined his mission when he said, "The Son of Man has come to seek and save that which is lost" (Luke 19:10). And again when he said, "For the Son of Man has come not to be ministered unto, but to minister and to give his life a ransom for many" (Mark 10:45). Then he added, "As my Father hath sent me, even so send I you" (John 20:21). So, his mission is our mission.

In the classic film, "Annie Hall," Woody Allen interrupts the deranged ramblings of his girlfriend's brother by saying, "Excuse me, but I have an appointment back on planet Earth."

That's us! We have an appointment, a divine appointment, on planet Earth. It was made for us 2,000 years ago on the Mount of Olives when Jesus said, "Go ye therefore and teach all nations, baptizing them in the name of the Father, and of the Son, and of the Holy Ghost: Teaching them to observe all things whatsoever I have commanded you: and, lo, I am with you alway, even unto the end of the world" (Matt. 28:19-20). Our assignment begins at the end of our nose and our toes, and it goes and grows until it penetrates the whole world for Christ.

The church is the ultimate institution God has chosen to reach and disciple the world. It is the only existing institution which witnesses to the spiritual and the eternal. God created it for the redemption of mankind and to be a witness to the coming kingdom.

A psychiatrist once described the church as a hypochondriac widow living behind closed blinds with the memories of her dead husband. A hypochondriac, by dictionary definition, is one who exhibits "morbid anxiety over one's own health." That's an apt description of many churches, large and small.

It's tragic when a church turns inward and thinks only of itself; when consciously or unconsciously it ceases to care about growth, to be friendly, to reach out to its community. To remain vital and dynamic a church must always look beyond itself and reach out to the lost world for Christ.

Bill O'Brien, missionary and missions executive, related that several years ago a documentary film was shown on Russian television that had lain on the KGB censorship shelves for years. The title of the film: "Repentance."

Toward the end of the film a little babushka (grandmother) moves out into a deserted street, looking confused. She looks up and down. Finally she encountered a soldier and asked him, "Where is the church? Where are the churches?" He replied, "There is no church. There are no churches." To which she asked, "What good is a street that doesn't lead to a church?"

O'Brien then turned the question around and asked, "What good is a church that doesn't lead to the street?" Well?

A church exists by mission like a fire exists by burning. When a fire stops burning it goes out. It dies. And when a church loses its sense of mission, then that church begins to die also, no matter what size it is. It may continue to meet, it may have all the outward signs of life, but for all practical purposes spiritual rigor mortis has begun.

To remain vibrant and alive the church must retain its sense of mission. We can't, therefore, be content to sit behind the desk and play solitaire with the prospect cards. We must, as William Booth said, "Go after souls and go after the worst of them."

The Organization vs. the Cause

One of the dangers churches must guard against, especially older churches, whether they are large or small, is letting the organization become more important than the cause, i.e., the buildings or the programs or the traditions of the church becoming more important than the mission of the church.

There's a way to check whether this has happened. Ask yourself, "What is sacred around here? What is there that you don't touch, that you don't change?"

In the Old Testament the ark of the covenant was sacred. The ark of the covenant was a highly ornate box that contained the tablets of the Ten Commandments, a pot of manna, and Aaron's rod that budded. It was considered the seat, the very dwelling place, of God. It was so holy that no person should touch it.

Mounted on each of the four corners of the ark were rings. Staves were placed through the rings so the priests could carry it on their shoulders without touching it. If a person touched the ark of the covenant he died (Num. 4:15).

In David's day the ark was rescued from the Philistines and was being taken to Jerusalem on an ox cart. The rough road so shook the ark that it was about to slide off the cart. Uzzah reached up to steady it and he died the instant he touched it (2 Sam. 6:6-7).

In every church there are certain things untouchable. If you try to change them, you're a goner. It may be the music ministry. It may be the older ladies' Sunday School class. It may be the furniture in the foyer, given in memory of someone. It may be the pulpit. One of the first things a pastor ought to do when he goes to a new church is to find out what is sacred, what is not to be touched.

Nothing, and I do mean nothing, ought to be sacred in a church except the Lord himself and the gospel. But there will be. And when too many things and too many places become untouchable, the organization is in danger of becoming more important than the cause, and the vitality of the church is in jeopardy.

Someone to Look Up To

Many of our churches today, especially older and smaller ones, are in trouble. According to the late Ray Steadman, 85 percent of all churches have either plateaued or are declining. The hard fact is that the average growth cycle of a church is only 12 to 15 years. After that almost all of them struggle just to hold their own.

The key to a church staying on mission and maintaining its vitality over the years is the pastor. He charts the course. He verbalizes the mission. He sets the tone. I will deal extensively with pastoral leadership in the next chapter, but for now it is sufficient to say that the church never rises above the vision of its pastor. If he doesn't challenge the people and lead them forward, they will sit and do nothing and do it very well until Jesus comes. In fact, most of the churches I have pastored did nothing better than they did anything else.

We must not let the church's limitations determine our expectations. We must, in the words of William Carey, "Expect great things from God and attempt great things for God." We must think big and dream big even though the church may be small.

Twice the Bible encourages us to learn from the ant (Prov. 6:6; 30:25). They have a lot to teach us. I read recently about two ants that lived on a golf course. One day a golfer drove his ball down the fairway and it landed on the ant hill where they lived. When he reached his ball he drew back his club, took a mighty sweep at the ball, and missed it completely. But he killed half the ants that lived on the hill. He drew his club back again, took another mighty swing, and missed again. This time he killed all but two of the remaining ants. One of them said to the other, "Joe, if we're going to survive this thing we'd better get on the ball."

So must we.

You Can Make a Difference

The Bible tells us that Christ loved the church and gave himself for it. That makes the church, every church, important, including yours. It has a mission to accomplish, a role to fill, a work to do, no matter what size it is. And, since everything in life is a process of radiation, you and your church can start where you are and affect the whole world. The poet put it this way:

> *One man awake can awaken another.*
> *And the second can waken his next door brother.*
> *And the three awake can waken the town*
> *By turning the whole place upside down.*
> *The many awake can make such a fuss*
> *That it finally awakens the rest of us.*
> *One man up with dawn in his eyes*
> *Multiplies.*

The Hallmark Hall of Fame made-for-television movie, "An American Story," is about several World War II veterans from an imaginary small town in Texas who had been a part of the same unit in the war. Following their discharge, they returned home to Ovington, Texas, to rebuild their lives.

George, who had been the commander of the unit, joined his father's law practice. A local political boss urged George to be the party's candidate in an upcoming election. He said to him, "We need a fighting man the people can look up to."

George responded, "I'm not a fighting man any more. I'm tired. All I'm looking for is a place to lie down. And, it's hard to look up to someone taking a nap."

Pastor, if your church is asleep, you're the one who needs to wake up. Nodding churches need wide-awake leaders. Get a vision of what you think the church ought to do. Dream big dreams. Develop a strategy for getting it done and go to work at accomplishing it. Give your people someone to look up to and something to look forward to. Remember the motto, "If it's to be, it's up to me." Revival and renewal have to start somewhere. Why not let them start with you?

On April 19, 1775, seventy-seven minutemen were lined up on the Lexington Green outside Boston, Massachusetts. Up came the British commander riding ahead of six companies of British infantry — 800 men. The British moved smartly into position, just 150 feet from the minutemen.

The British major yelled out, "Curse ye damned rebels, disperse ye villains! Lay down your arms." Captain John Parker, commander of the minutemen, walked along behind his men and said, "Don't fire unless fired upon, but if they mean to have war, let it begin here."

If we're going to turn things around in our churches and in our world, it has to start with someone, somewhere. I say, "Why not here? Why not now? Why not with you?"

You don't have to be in a big place to do a big work for God. You and your church can make a difference.

Chapter 2

It Takes a Big Man to Lead a Smaller Church

Being a pastor is a tough assignment anywhere, anytime. But the challenge of pastoring a smaller church is the toughest of all. That's why I believe it takes a big man to lead a smaller church. It takes a man big in faith, big in vision, big in dedication, and big in leadership.

Why is this true? It is because he often is confronted with changing neighborhoods and unchanging attitudes. He has to work with volunteer help over which he has no authority. And he has to operate on free will offerings over which he has no control. He has to motivate untrained leadership and manage limited resources. And all the while he must rock the boat just enough to keep the passengers awake but not so much as to tip it over, remembering the words of the late Fred Swank, "It's easier to throw you out of a small boat than it is out of a large one."

The smaller church is clearly no place for ministerial midgets. And, this is definitely no time for them. Paul

Harvey put it this way, "When small men cast long shadows the sun is about to set."

Winston Churchill once said to the Israeli army, "The first right of a soldier is the right to a competent commander." Every church, I believe, has that same right.

One thing is for sure, the church will never rise above the dreams and vision of its leadership. No organization or movement ever does. In real estate the important thing is location, location, location. In the church it's leadership! leadership! leadership!

Tony Campolo said there are more pastors holding churches back than there are churches holding pastors back. That's due in part to the fact that many pastors do not know the difference between management and leadership. Management is maintaining the organization, keeping the programs and machinery running. Leadership is different. Leadership is getting a vision of what the Lord wants his church to do, developing a strategy for doing it, and then motivating the people to join in doing it. That's what every church needs, no matter what size it is.

What are the qualities of good leadership in the church and especially a smaller church? I share 12 with you:

Are You for Real?

The first quality of a good leader is integrity. Leading a church, pastoring the people, and being a good preacher are not isolated events. They cannot be separated from who and what we are. Aristotle said 2,300 years ago, "The impact of a message often depends on who said it. We believe good men more readily than others."

What is integrity? It is the quality of being able to be

trusted. It means we don't lie to each other. What we say we do, the affection we possess is genuine and the praise we give is honest.

New York City Mayor Ed Koch once said of Donald Trump, "I wouldn't believe Donald Trump if he had his tongue notarized." If people ever get the idea you can't be trusted, you're dead in the water as a leader.

A pastor I know left his church after a long and effective ministry. He was followed by a man whose integrity soon became suspect. Some of the people were critical of him. Another member, trying to support his new pastor, said, "But not everyone loved our former pastor." A relatively new Christian responded by saying, "No, not everyone loved him. But everyone respected him."

No pastor can have everyone love him, but he had better have everyone respect him. If the people ever discover that you don't practice what you preach, that you are not a person of character, you will lose your leadership.

General H. Norman Schwarzkopf was on target when he said, "Leadership is a potent combination of strategy and character. But if you must be without one, be without the strategy."

I preached once at the First Baptist Church of Charleston, South Carolina. Following the sermon a lady came to me and asked, "Are you for real?" I think she wanted to know if I was sincere, if I really believed what I was saying. She was going through a tough time in her marriage and wanted to know if I really believed what I had just preached. That's what people always want to know of their leaders.

James Stewart, the great Scottish teacher in Edinburgh,

said, "God does not need your eloquence. He does not need your cleverness. God does not need your showmanship. God does not need your impressive subjects. Above everything else, God needs you to be real."

That's a quality of good leadership that the church deserves.

Where There Is No Vision

The second quality of a good church leader is vision. Warren Bennis stated that the single defining quality of a leader is vision. A leader is one who is in tune with the future, who knows where God wants him to go, a person who is focused on a clear purpose. As one person put it, a leader sees more than others, farther than others, and before others.

Studies conducted on growing churches around the nation indisputably indicate that vision and passion are two central elements in attracting people to a church and to faith in Jesus Christ. The Bible says, "Where there is no vision, the people perish" (Prov. 29:18). The opposite is also true. Where there is vision, the people flourish.

Someone said, "Our preachers aren't dreaming. That's why the church is such a nightmare." Pastor, if your church is asleep, you are the one who needs to wake up . . . and start dreaming. Carl Sandburg was right, "Nothing happens unless it's first a dream."

The right of every congregation is to have a person of vision as their leader.

The Right Headquarters

The third quality of good leadership is wisdom. There is a difference between wisdom and intelligence. Intelligence implies a degree of knowledge and the ability to learn. Wisdom has to do with judgment. One of the great obstacles the North faced in winning the war between the states was the ineptness of its generals. They were uniformly good men, but they lacked either intelligence or courage in battle. When Burnside fought the battle at Fredericksburg he lost 15,000 dead and wounded. Lincoln blamed himself because he allowed Burnside to talk him into attacking. He said, "This is madness, attacking in the wintertime, across the river, when the entire Confederate army is entrenched."

"Burnside insisted, you must understand; I gave way. You must give way to a general who fights." One of his aides responded, "Fights, yes, but does not think."

In the midst of one battle, General "Fighting Joe" Hooker sent President Lincoln the message: "Hindquarters in the saddle." This prompted Lincoln to say, "The trouble with Hooker is that his headquarters are where his hindquarters ought to be."

A good leader must be right most of the time or the people will lose confidence in him. And a part of wisdom is to know what to do, to know who to listen to, to know what to attempt, and to know what to leave alone.

Put Their Interests First

The fourth quality of good leadership is compassion. A Christian leader must really care about people. Mark it down somewhere, people don't care how much you know until they know how much you care. If you put their best interest first they will follow you. But if they ever get the idea you are serving your own interests they will turn from you. So be sensitive to your people, care about their feelings. Talk with them. It's a part of really caring.

If ever there was a leader, it was General George Patton. Some of the general's leadership tactics were controversial, but it should be remembered that, as a wartime executive, General Patton had to lead "under fire" in the truest sense of the term. It also should be noted that the general achieved most of his rank during peacetime service — an accomplishment that must be credited to the qualities of a good leader.

One of Patton's first rules was, "Make sure you speak to your soldiers, because they are the ones doing the fighting."

Porter Williamson puts it this way in his book, *General Patton: Principles for Life and Leadership:* "During staff meetings, General Patton would instruct, 'Always talk with the troops! They know more about the war than anybody. Make them tell you all of their gripes. Talk with them. Always remember when talking with the troops, the most important thing to do is to listen.'"

Are you talking with your troops? Above all, are you listening? You must care enough to do both if you are going to be a good leader. Take time this next week and consciously observe yourself "talking with the troops" and listening to what they have to say. It might come in handy if you want to win an important battle. It for sure will save you some headaches and some heartache.

When King Solomon came to the end of his reign, he was a very unpopular leader. He had overtaxed the people and been abusive and inconsiderate in his dealings with them. At his death, Rehoboam, his son, was to succeed him. Before anointing him as king, Israel met with him at Shechem and wanted to know his leadership style.

Rehoboam wisely asked for three days to consider his answer. He consulted first with the older, wiser men of Israel. They suggested that he needed to lighten up, that they needed a kinder, gentler administration.

Then he consulted with the younger men, those with whom he had grown up. They said, "Bo, don't knuckle under. Don't show a sign of weakness. Show 'em who's boss."

So, Rehoboam ignored the advice of the older men and followed the advice of the younger. He told Israel his father had beaten them with whips, but he would beat them with scorpions. He said my finger will be heavier than my father's thigh. Not listening to the advice of the wise, older men, not really caring about them, he followed the advice of his peers and he split the kingdom. If you, as pastor of a smaller church, ignore a major segment of your church, especially the older, wiser people, you will split your church also.

Don't Be a Wimp

The fifth quality of a good leader is courage. Former president George Bush once referred to a well-known politician as "Senator Straddle." You can't be a great leader in the church and straddle the fence. You've got to have the courage of your convictions. You've got to stand up and speak out. Always with sensitivity, as I just said, but you must speak up nonetheless. If you are determined to be wishy-washy on the hard issues of life, don't expect people to follow you. As Forrest Gump said, "If you can't stand the heat, get out of the oven."

I had breakfast once with a man in a church where I was interim. The pulpit committee had announced to the congregation that the next Sunday their new prospective pastor would preach in view of a call. He said to me, "I sure hope he's not a wimp. I've had enough wimps for pastors."

Men won't follow a wimp. But you surely don't need to be a bully either. And you don't need to abuse the people. You do, however, have to be convinced in your heart that a thing is right and then say so. You should never get mad if the people don't agree or if they vote you down, but they need to know what you think. There is a difference between leadership and lordship. You can be dominant without being domineering.

Winston Churchill said, "An army of lions led by a sheep is no match for an army of sheep led by a lion." Be as bold as a lion in your leadership, but as gentle as a lamb in your relationships.

Fired with Enthusiasm

The sixth quality of a good leader is enthusiasm. If you can't get excited about what you are doing, don't expect the people to either. The people catch your spirit the same way they catch your cold, by getting close to you.

Our enthusiasm comes from our dreams. You can't get excited about nothing. Dreams and goals wake us up and get us up. When my son was in the second grade, his class planned to go on a field trip to nearby Austin. He, like any eight-year-old, was hard to get up in the mornings. I usually had to call him several times to get him out of bed. The day before his field trip he said to me, "Dad, tomorrow morning all you need to do is whisper in my ear, 'Austin!' and I'll get up."

The next morning I leaned over his bed, whispered in his ear, "Mike, Austin!" He was up in a flash. He had something he wanted to do, he was excited about it, and hopped right out of bed. His anticipation motivated him. I went to his room the next morning, leaned over the bed and whispered in his ear, "Austin!" Nothing happened. I said, "San Antonio! Dallas! Houston! Fayetteville!" He turned over and said sleepily, "Ah, Dad."

Dreams awaken us, no matter what age we are. But without dreams there will be no excitement and without excitement there will be no leadership.

Dr. Clark Kerr, director of the Carnegie Commission on Higher Education, recalling his dismissal as president of the University of California, said, "I left the presidency as I entered it — fired with enthusiasm."

I hope it can be said of us — that we leave the ministry as we entered it — enthusiastic for God and for his work.

Tell the People to Go Forward

The seventh quality of a good leader is initiative. Good leaders are proactive, not reactive. They challenge the people to go forward. F. B. Thorne, who pastored First Baptist Church of Wichita, Kansas, was a great church builder. His motto was, "Do right and go forward." This was the word of God to Moses and the Israelites when they stopped moving forward from Egypt to Canaan. The Israelites were grumbling to Moses, "Didn't we say to you in Egypt, 'Leave us alone; let us serve the Egyptians?' It would have been better for us to serve the Egyptians than to die in the desert." Moses answered the people, "Do not be afraid. Stand firm and you will see the deliverance the Lord will bring to you today. The Egyptians you see today you will never see again. The Lord will fight for you; you need only to be still." Then the Lord said to Moses, "Why are you crying out to me? Tell the Israelites to move on."

Sitting on the status quo . . . standing pat . . . doing nothing always seems easier and less costly. But it will never work in building a church or building the kingdom of God. Leaders get a vision from God, develop a strategy for fulfilling that vision, and challenge the people to go forward.

We need the resolve of David Livingston who said, "I'm willing to go anywhere, so long as it's forward."

A Towel, Not a Scepter

The eighth quality of a good leader is humility. You need a servant spirit. Nowhere in the Bible does the Lord ever speak of "Moses, my leader" or "Joshua, my leader." It is always, "Moses, my servant" and "Joshua, my servant."

We are servant leaders. In the upper room Jesus washed the disciples' feet. When he had finished he said, "Do you realize what has happened here tonight?" They weren't the sharpest group ever assembled. So he said, "You call me Master and Lord: and you say well; for so I am. If I, then, your Lord and Master, have washed your feet; you also ought to wash one another's feet. For I have given you an example that you should do as I have done to you" (John 13:13-15). This is the only place in the Bible where Jesus said, "I have given you an example."

Then he gave us a beatitude. He said, "If you know

these things, happy are you if you do them" (v. 17). I fully believe one of the reasons there is so much unhappiness in the ministry today is that we've traded the towel for a scepter. We want to be rulers rather than servants.

In this experience, Jesus humbled himself and assumed the role of a common slave by washing their feet. He became their servant. Leaders who follow his example will have followers who trust and serve because they see Christ in their pastor.

No matter how noble the motive, however, when a pastor trades the towel of a servant for the whip of a tyrant, he will eventually wound the very people he is called to feed and nurture. A pastor who exercises control over the congregation through fear and intimidation makes a mockery of Christ's servant leadership style.

In a Hurry

The ninth quality of a good leader is a sense of urgency. Henry Kaiser was a great industrialist. He was always in a hurry. He had a sense of urgency about what he was doing. One of his men said to him on one occasion, "Henry, remember Rome wasn't built in a day." He said, "I know, but I wasn't on that project."

In 1266, the great Mongolian empire, led by Kublai Khan, stretched from the Black Sea to the Pacific Ocean. It was a crucial time, as the faith of Islam hung by a thread among the nations. That year Kublai Khan sent word to Marco Polo for the Christian church in Rome to send 100 men to teach Christianity to his court.

It could have been a turning point in the history of the faith. But the church members at Rome were so busy fighting among themselves that it was 28 years before one — not 100 — reached the Mongol court. Already retired, Kublai Khan said, "It's too late! I have grown old in my idolatry."

These are urgent and demanding times. We must be persons of urgency.

Light and Bugs

The tenth quality of a good leader is persistency. A leader must have an amazing tolerance for criticism and rejection. The idea that leaders have universal appeal is a myth. No leader has ever had universal appeal. No pastor has ever had universal support. Even Paul was stoned by his enemies and Jesus was crucified by his. Leadership does not mean we have everyone's support. Leadership is the ability to keep going even when we have little or no support.

Remember this: where there is light, there will be bugs. All great leaders have faced obstacles and opposition. They succeed only by persisting.

M. A. Gruder, administrator of the supersonic transport program of the Department of Transportation, reminds us, "To be successful in Washington you must have the ability to lay a firm foundation with the bricks others throw at you." That's true everywhere. Even if you're in God's service, there will always be some Pharaoh on your trail, some Jezebel to hound, some Goliath to taunt. The successful leader goes on in spite of opposition.

Don't Forget to Laugh

The eleventh essential to being a good leader is a sense of humor. You can't take the work of the Lord too seriously, but you can take yourself too seriously. Some preachers act as if they are so holy they wouldn't take any-thing but St. Joseph's aspirin. Pastor, relax! Enjoy your-self and enjoy the people and enjoy the Lord. Lighten up. You'll be a better leader.

I just returned from the funeral service of Dr. Abner V. McCall, longtime president of Baylor University and one of our most distinguished Baptist leaders of this genera-tion. Six religious and political leaders, who had known "The Judge" for years, spoke during the service. To a man they mentioned his sense of humor as one of the things that made him great. He always took his work seriously, but he never took himself too seriously.

Viktor Frankl, the Swiss psychiatrist who endured the atrocities of a German concentration camp, wrote a book, *Man's Search for Meaning*. He studied the lives of people who had survived concentration camps and said, "I learned that the people who were most likely to survive were those who had a sense of humor."

It's hard to imagine finding anything amusing in a con-centration camp. And it's hard to find much amusing in a deacons' meeting at times. But the people who survive and thrive in the ministry, as well as those who survived concentration camps, are those who keep their sense of humor.

Be an Example

The twelfth quality of an effective Christian leader is example. We must practice what we preach. We must show the people how to do it. If you're going to lead peo-ple to go forward, you must go forward yourself. If you are going to lead them to visit, you must be out visiting. If you're going to lead them to be sacrificial in their giving, you must sacrifice.

In time people know what you are. If you are living in an ivory tower, not out among the people, not doing the work, not making a sacrifice, don't expect them to. Leaders lead by example.

That's what leadership in the smaller church is all about: integrity, vision, wisdom, compassion, courage, enthusiasm, initiative, humility, urgency, persistency, humor, and example.

Russian empress Catherine the Great, during her changing times in the eighteenth century, said, "A great wind is blowing and that gives you either imagination or a headache."

Great winds of change are blowing today. If the church is to have a bright future it must have the right leaders. Will you be one of them?

Chapter 3

Holy Sweat

Leadership in the church is not like leadership in any other place — not like corporate America, not like the military, not like athletics. Leadership in the church is not demanded or commanded. You get it the old fashioned way — you earn it. You earn it by the hard work of being a good pastor. You earn it by holy sweat.

In the smaller church arena, more than any other, leadership grows out of relationships. If people know you, love you, trust you, and are convinced you have their best interests at heart, they will listen to you and follow you. So, the quickest and surest way to establish yourself as a leader is to go to work at your pastoral duties.

Be among the people. Get to know them. Be interested in them. Be a loving shepherd. That's one of the most important things any preacher can do. Orville Scott, coordinator of news/information for the Baptist General Convention of Texas, expressed this beautifully in a poem:

Some are given a golden voice
That helps them be the people's choice
And some can write with golden pen
To move the hearts of calloused men,
But of all the works of the Master's art,
The greatest to me is a caring heart.

We can't all be eloquent preachers. We can't all be dynamic leaders. But we can all have caring hearts. We can all be good ministers. And that, after all, is what we've been called to be.

A smaller church affords a special opportunity to develop a pastoral ministry and to build the kind of relationships that make effective leadership possible. In a smaller church there are not so many members that the pastor cannot know them all and there are not so many demands on his time that he does not have time to care for them all. So the smaller church affords the best opportunity you will ever have to be a servant leader.

A couple of years ago the Dallas Cowboys played the Detroit Lions. Michael Irvin, the all-pro wide receiver, missed the team plane for the game. He took a later flight and arrived in time for the kick-off, but he had violated the team rules so coach Jimmy Johnson fined him $1,000 and made him sit out the first series of the game.

Afterwards, reporters questioned him as to why he missed the flight. He told him it was none of their business. Then he said, "They pay me to catch the ball. That's all."

The next day a sports writer quoted Irvin and then noted, "They don't just pay Michael to catch footballs. They pay him to catch planes also."

Some pastors want to live in an ivory tower. They want to preach and administer the church program, but they don't want to be bothered with people. But I remind you, your church, especially if it is a smaller church, called you and pays you not just to preach and lead, but also to minister to people. It called you as pastor, as its shepherd. And anyone who takes upon himself a profession must take all phases of it — the bad with the good, the sacrifices with the benefits, the cost with the profits. The lawyer must defend, the doctor must tend the sick, the pastor must serve.

To be an effective pastor in a smaller church there are several things you ought to do.

The Way to Get Close

First, you ought to visit in the home of every member of your congregation. Occasionally a young minister asks me how to begin a new ministry. My advice is always the same: begin among the people. Make it a point to be in the home of every member of your congregation during your first year if at all possible.

This is what I did in the first four churches I pastored. I began this practice at Belfalls. With only 20-30 families in the church it was relatively easy. I continued the practice at Troy. There we had about 100 families, and again it was not hard. At Taylor, with approximately 200 families, and at San Marcos, with around 400 families, it became more difficult, but I did it. At Tyler, with around 700 families and rapid growth, it became virtually impossible. Through home visitation I got to know the people and I won the admiration of many who had never had a pastor visit in their home. You can do the same thing.

While a student at Southwestern Baptist Theological Seminary I read a good word from Andrew Blackwood. He said, "A home going pastor makes for a church going people." That has proven true in my experience.

The first thing some pastors want to do when they go to a church is reorganize the Sunday School, "whip the deacons into line," institute a purchase order system, or rewrite the church constitution. My advice is, don't tamper with the structure of the church until you have been there for some time and unless you plan to stay. And if you start too soon you might not last as long as you had hoped.

Churches are, understandably, reluctant to change. Many smaller churches change pastors every 18-20 months, and every new pastor wants to make changes. Then just about the time he gets things changed and the members thoroughly upset, he moves on. Then, in comes another pastor who starts the process over again. Little wonder that change is not always welcome.

Furthermore, change will accomplish little unless you stay a long time, for as soon as you leave, the church will revert to its old ways of operating. What's important to remember is that the Lord called us to change people, not to change structures.

How can we best do that? Howard Hendricks said, "You can impress people at a distance, but you impact people up close." I found home visitation the best way to get close to people in a hurry.

So, in a smaller church, and even in a large one, spend your first year getting to know your people, winning the lost, and preaching your best. Pastors rarely encounter trouble when they follow these priorities.

Give Them Intensive Care

Second, to be an effective pastor in a smaller church, pay special attention to special needs. The local church should be a general hospital where each member receives intensive care. The sick, the elderly, the bereaved should always have special attention.

The way you care for these people not only indicates your concern for them, but like it or not, it often determines how much they feel God cares. If you don't care about them and minister to them, they may wonder if God cares.

A young man I know was the victim of a senseless assault years ago. He has been comatose since that time and will probably remain so the rest of his life. A new pastor, who came to his church shortly after the tragedy, told the family he would faithfully minister to them. Though he drove by their home on a regular basis he never stopped. The family became bitter and disillusioned.

Fortunately, others reached out to them. Then, just recently, the young man's mother wrote this note to her former pastor: "May is a hard month for me. It is the month Mike was injured and the month when my mother died. You, Ron, and a young man from Southside made me see that God had not forgotten me."

Do you see what she was saying? Her pastor neglected her and she felt God had forgotten her. We do represent the Lord and the way we treat people reflects on him.

The elderly, especially shut-ins, need special attention. And, by the way, senior adults are some of the easiest people for a new pastor to win over. They respond readily to a little attention and they quickly love the new pastor who cares enough to visit them and pay a little attention to them.

Busier Than You Ought to Be

Third, to be an effective pastor in a smaller church, be available to your people. Julia Ward Howe, the writer of "The Battle Hymn of the Republic," went to nineteenth century statesman, Charles Sumner, to plead for help for a needy family. Sumner replied, "Julia, I have become so busy I cannot concern myself with individuals." When that happens to us, we are busier than God intended us to be.

B. H. Carroll said one night he read the four gospels and noted the times people tried to get an audience with Jesus — either one person or a group. Carroll noted that there were at least 150 times when someone sought Jesus . . . and not once was anyone turned away. It can be exhausting, but if we are going to be good ministers, we must have that same availability.

In a smaller church, if your study is not at the church, move it there. Establish regular office hours. Show up on time. Let the people know that you're not sleeping late or sitting around the house drinking coffee and reading the paper. Be available to them. Don't get so bogged down in administrative work or even in sermon preparation that you have no time for your people.

Admiral Hyman G. Rickover said, "After the end of World War I, a commission was set up by the Weimar Republic to study and report on the cause of Germany's defeat. The commission found that a major cause of this defeat was the amount of paperwork required by the armed forces. Toward the end, they were literally buried in paper." (*U.S. News and World Report* 9/30/68.)

If you aren't careful you too can get so buried in administration, even in a smaller church, that you have no time for the real work of God — serving his people. And, as a result, you may lose more than a war.

Don't Leave Anyone Out

Fourth, to be an effective minister in a smaller church, visit everyone in your area, no matter who they are. From 1923 to 1955, Robert Woodruff was president of Coca-Cola Bottling Company. After World War II he led the company to adopt his goal. Woodruff's goal, succinctly stated, was, "During my lifetime I want every person in the world to taste Coca-Cola." If a businessman can dream about the whole world tasting his product in his lifetime, shouldn't a pastor dream of giving every person in his community a chance to taste the "living water" during his ministry in a place? So in a smaller place visit everyone. Witness to everybody. Don't leave anyone out.

At Belfalls, where I began pastoring, I asked one of my deacons to draw me a map locating every farm in the community and identifying the people who lived there. On Sunday afternoons I went visiting. I drove down every road, stopped at every house, talked to every person in the community. It didn't matter to me what church they were a member of. Ours was the only church in the countryside and I wanted them to know they were welcome.

As a result, we baptized more people the year and a half I pastored there than anyone in the church could ever remember. We didn't have a baptistry in our church so we used the baptistry of the First Baptist Church of Troy, six miles away. We actually used their baptistry more than they did, so when they lost their pastor they called me. Visitation pays in more ways than one.

People appreciated my hard work and my spirit and it affected their spirit and attitude also. In a small community word always gets around. It will get around about you also. And what they say will greatly determine your effectiveness.

I followed the same ministry pattern in Troy, my second pastorate. It was, at that time, a small town with a population of 400. I started at the end of one street, knocked on the first door, introduced myself as the new preacher in town, and invited them to church. If they said they attended one of the other three churches in town, I expressed my joy and told them if I could ever be of help to them to feel free to call me. I then went to the house next door and did the same thing. I kept it up until I had visited every home in town.

I then went down every country road and visited every farm house within miles of our community. I often took Jack Dooley, Sr., the owner of the local grocery store, as my visitation partner. He already knew everyone in the countryside and they knew him, so he was a great asset.

Once again, word got around about my visitation and about the church. Naturally it created a lot of good will and laid a good foundation for me and for the church, both of which helped me the entire five years I was there.

My next pastorate was Taylor, Texas, a town of 10,000 population. I wasn't able to visit everyone in the city, but I did cover about one-third of it during my five year pastorate. And I did it by going house to house, door to door, "cold turkey," as they say.

The benefits of this kind of visitation are untold.

- You win some people to the Lord.
- You discover new prospects.
- You plant seeds for a later harvest.
- You encourage some people to begin attending their own church again.
- You build good will in the community.
- You establish relationships with unchurched people who will call you later when they have special needs, such as a marriage, a death in the family or a child in trouble.
- You understand the community better.
- You set an example for your people and make them proud of you.

Let me cite three examples of my visitation in Taylor that bear this out. One day I approached a house that was little more than a shack. My first thought was, "No one lives here so I won't even stop." Then I thought, "No, I am going to knock on every door in town." So I stopped. An elderly lady in a clean, but threadbare and faded, dress answered the door. I introduced myself, asked if she went to church, and gave a brief witness for Christ. She told me she didn't go to church but would if she had adequate clothes. I told her if she really wanted to attend church I would see that she had the clothes. So, I called one of our widows who lived down the street and told her the story. The next Sunday the widow brought the prospect to church in her new clothes. The following Thursday I called on the lady again to appeal to her to accept Christ as her personal Savior. She readily responded and as I was rising to leave she said, "Pastor, I'll be in church again Sunday and make my profession of faith. Then I want you to baptize me."

On Saturday night she died. Monday I buried her — in her new clothes and as a new Christian. My visit was a divine appointment, I am persuaded.

I called on another home that had a mother and her two teenage children, and the grandmother. I was met with indifference and apathy. But a month later the mother was involved in a serious automobile accident that left her bedridden for several weeks. Guess who the family called requesting prayer? That's right! The only pastor who had ever visited and witnessed to them. During the convalescent period I visited the family several times. When the mother was well she, her two children, and the grandmother all began attending our church and in time I baptized the mother, the two teenagers, and received the grandmother by transfer of letter.

Another day I stopped at a house and visited the man of the house who was working in his yard. He was a Methodist who had dropped out of the church several years earlier. I greeted him and engaged him in a brief conversation about Christ and the church. I encouraged him to get back into fellowship with the Lord and begin attending church again and then moved on. A few weeks later the man was again working in his yard when I walked by. He yelled out at me, "Hey, preacher, I started back to my church last week."

Barbara Cunningham, who teaches in Billy Graham schools of evangelism, tells her classes about the time she and her preacher husband, Milton, went to serve in a church where the previous pastor had distanced himself from the people. He had told them they should not call him at home. If they needed him they could reach him at his office Monday through Friday from 9:00 a.m. to 5:00 p.m. The results of this announcement was that the people felt, and rightly so, that the pastor didn't want to be bothered with them.

Milton and Barbara felt if they were to change things in the church it would need to begin in their home. So they developed what they called their "ABC Plan". They went down the church roll and invited groups of people in alphabetical order to their home for a Sunday evening get-acquainted visit.

People do not go to Sunday School alphabetically and they do not sit in church alphabetically so their ABC plan not only brought people to their house they didn't know; it also brought people together who didn't know one another. Barbara did the calling. She asked them to come to their home at 8:30 on Sunday night but said nothing about it being after church. Some of the people were suspicious and hesitant. One lady said, "But we don't attend church on Sunday night." Barbara said, "That doesn't matter, come anyhow." The lady then asked, "Is the pastor going to ask my husband for money?" Barbara assured her that this was just to get to know them better.

She always invited twice as many as she expected because some people did not show up. It took several years to go through the entire church roll but they said it was one of the best relationship building things they ever did.

A pastor's wife who heard Barbara tell this story later

related that she thought, "We have only 50 people in our church. We could have every one of them in our home the first month." So she and her husband decided to invite the whole community to their home.

They, of course, served in a small community and using the telephone directory invited everyone in town to their home over a period of time. She later told Barbara that among other things this had helped to break down both denominational and racial prejudices in the community. After all, people aren't listed in the phone book by their religious denomination or the color of their skin.

These are wonderful ideas that can work in lots of churches — large and small.

If you're going to be effective as the pastor of a smaller church, you need to ring door bells, as well as church bells. I determined a long time ago that if no one else in the church did what they ought to do, I would. And, I realized early on, there was a greater probability of others going to work for Christ if they first knew I was working.

By the way, the worse the weather, the better time it is to visit. When it's stormy, snowing, sleeting, or raining, go visiting. That's when you're most likely to find your prospects at home. When I was pastor in Tyler, I had tried unsuccessfully, on several occasions, to catch an oilman at home. One Thursday afternoon it began snowing. It seldom snowed in east Texas, but that afternoon it really came down. I figured he'd be home so I drove to his house. When I arrived, he was in the front yard playing with his boys. As I got out of the car he said, "Preacher, what are you doing out on a day like this?" I replied,

"Friend, I'm out because you're in." The next Sunday he was in church.

Be a Worker

Any way you cut it, it takes hard work to be a good pastor of a smaller church. In fact, toil and labor are at the heart of effective service for our Lord anytime, anywhere. They always have been.

God's work is holy, but it is also hard. It is glorious, but it can also be grueling. As often as not it comes down to blood and sweat and tears.

General George Patton is my military hero. Once, while encouraging his troops to train hard for approaching combat duty, he said, "A little sweat now will save you a lot of blood later."

That's good advice for the pastors of smaller churches also. So, pastor, put some holy sweat into your pastoring, especially early in your ministry, and it will save you a lot of blood and tears later.

Chapter 4

Worship: Feeling Good or Finding God

The quickest and perhaps the easiest way for a pastor to influence a church is through the worship service. It is the one time when all the church is together in one place. It is the one time when the pastor is most in control of what happens. It is the one time when he has the ear of all the people. In time, the worship service will inevitably take on the flavor of his personality. So, the pastor who wants to change a church must pay attention to every phase of worship.

There is an emphasis on worship today such as I have not seen in my lifetime. But it is an unusual emphasis. It seems to be influenced more by the sociology of George Barna than the theology of the apostle Paul. Barna tells us that young people today are bored with traditional church approaches, standard worship services, and even sacred hymns. They are fascinated by fast moving, "Indiana Jones" type movies and want nonstop, secular-style services.

Unfortunately, for many people feeling good has become more important than finding God. And in an effort to reach them and build a big audience, many churches have discarded their hymnals and diluted their message. They have traded truth for therapy and have made preaching more psychological than theological. They are singing hand-clapping, toe-tapping, finger-snapping, knee-slapping music and preaching sermons geared to the felt needs of people. The result is they spend more time entertaining the goats than feeding the sheep.

I was preaching in the Dallas area recently and invited my son and his wife to attend the service. He told me they already planned to attend another church with a friend. The friend had said to him, "I think you'll like our church. It has a band and loud music. It's more like a show. It's fun. But it does have Christian overtones."

There is, of course, nothing wrong with entertainment, per se. And, going to church should be a happy experience. After all, the psalmist said, "I was glad when they said unto me, Let us go into the house of the Lord" (Ps. 122:1).

But there are subtle dangers in the consumer oriented, user-friendly entertainment approach to church. One is that it perverts the gospel. Neal Postman put his finger on this when he wrote, "I believe I'm not mistaken in saying that Christianity is a demanding and serious religion. When it is delivered as easy and amusing it is another kind of religion altogether."

Another danger with this approach to church is that it starts at the wrong place and ends up at the wrong place. Its aim is to please rather than to change people.

True worship starts with God, not with man — with

the Creator, not the creature — with the worshipped, not the worshipper.

God doesn't adapt in order to be worshipped. It is the worshipper who adapts in order to worship. Entering the sanctuary of God ought to be different from entering the coliseum or the supermarket or the theater.

We seemingly have lost our sense of reverence and awe in worship and we are trivializing God. The result is that the friends of Christ may be doing him more harm than his enemies, and the leaders of the church may be hurting it more than its critics.

The fact is, many of the lay people in our churches see through our "showmanship" and our "entertainment" better than we do. At the height of his popularity, a famous TV preacher had a member say, "I'm getting tired of our church being a circus before the whole world."

A word to the wise about worship: The goal of worship is not to meet needs, but to meet God, which is our greatest need. And, if you try to keep up with every new fad, read every new book, know and follow every new idea on how to do church, you'll go crazy. Anchor to something more permanent — anchor to the word of God. That's where we should get our concept of worship, not from contemporary culture.

A man once approached G. Campbell Morgan and said, "The preacher must catch the spirit of the age."

"God forgive him if he does," Morgan replied. "The preacher's job is to correct the spirit of the age."

The spirit of the age is a mixture of truth and falsehood. We go to church, in part, to receive truth that transcends the age. The gospel is to speak to this age and to resist fiercely a lot of the spirit of this age. If our faith is not greater and wiser than the insights of a particular age, what good is it?

We need to remember the words of Richard Emory, "If you marry the fad of your generation you will be a widow in the next." And, I am persuaded it will take us at least a generation to see the devastating effects of the consumer-oriented, need-centered, user-friendly emphasis that has captivated many churches today. And it won't be good.

An example of worship at its best is found in Isaiah 6. In the year king Uzziah died, Isaiah saw the Lord high and lifted up. His train filled the temple and the angels were singing, "Holy, holy, holy is the Lord of hosts" (Isa. 6:3).

As he saw the holiness of God he became aware of his own sinfulness and cried, "I am a man of unclean lips and live in the midst of a people of unclean lips" (Isa. 6:5). The angel of the Lord placed hot coals on his tongue as if to cleanse him of his sin.

Then he heard the voice of God, "Whom shall I send and who will go for me?" Isaiah responded, "Here am I, Lord, send me" (Isa. 6:8).

That's worship — seeing the glory of God, experiencing the cleansing of God, hearing the voice of God, and answering the call of God. Isaiah's experience was not characterized by the "Ho, ho, ho" of entertainment but by the "Woe, woe, woe" of divine encounter.

To introduce many of these new styles of worship in most traditional, smaller churches can be devastating. It can lead to dissatisfaction and conflict and in some cases termination. Pastors, especially of smaller churches with an older membership, must realize that the people of south

Chicago and southern California and the people of south Alabama are not alike. They are not only miles apart geographically but also culturally. What is acceptable in one place may very well not be acceptable in another.

I know the church must change, but not too much and not too fast. Since everything is changing I think one of the glories of the church is that it maintains a community which relates to the past. It means a lot to me today to go to church and sing the same hymns I sang as a child. And more than that, to sing some of the same hymns that my grandfather and his father before him sang.

Somehow we've got to move worship from the dead traditionalism and sterile ritualism that characterizes many churches to a dynamic, vital, meaningful encounter with God. There is enough dullness in the world already without the church adding to it. But we must change without turning everything upside down.

I'm convinced that it can be done. It is not so much what you do, as how you do it, that makes worship dynamic. You don't have to change the form so much as the spirit in which you do it. You can sing the old hymns if you sing them with new spirit. The fact is, we will still be singing the old hymns when the tubes of our overhead projectors have long since burned out. You can follow the same general order of service if you breathe new life into it. It is not the order we need to change but ourselves. It's not the program, but the people. Dry bones can live again. What we need to change is our spirit and our attitude and our participation more than anything else.

There are four essential ingredients to dynamic worship. The wise pastor will give attention to all of them.

They are:

- The preaching of God's word
- The singing of hymns
- Prayer
- The receiving of the offering

Baking Bread or Making Signs

The first ingredient of meaningful worship is preaching of God's word. For worship to be alive and dynamic the preaching must be good. By good I mean well prepared, well presented, biblical sermons. The revelation of God was complete in Jesus Christ. Jude speaks of the faith that was "once delivered unto the saints." The Greek word translated "once" literally means "once and for all."

God has revealed himself fully and finally in Christ. There is nothing to be added to or to be taken away from his revelation recorded in scripture. Thus, the Bible is the primary way God speaks to us today.

That revelation needs to be re-expressed, re-applied, and re-interpreted in every generation, but it cannot be added to. That's basically what good preaching does — it interprets and applies God's eternal truth to today's world.

The importance of preaching can not be over-estimated. The apostle Paul says, ". . . it pleased God by the foolishness of preaching to save them that believe" (I Cor. 1:21). When the gospel is preached in simplicity and in power, it is the most important thing that happens anywhere, anytime.

But in some cases, with the emphasis on marketing the church, preaching has been prostituted on the altar of public opinion and popular appeal. More and more we are being told we should preach "feel-good" sermons that address the "felt-needs." The result is that in some churches you are more apt to get a massage than a message. We are giving people psychological pabulum when what they need is gospel penicillin.

Gone, or fast going, are the classical themes of sin and repentance, God's wrath and judgment, sacrifice and service and being willing to suffer for the cause of Christ. Many preachers today have simply "air-brushed" sin out of their language. Their goal seems to be not to offend anyone, including the devil.

Every generation of preachers has faced the temptation to tell people what they want to hear. There have always been people who have wanted their ears tickled and there have always been preachers willing to tickle them. The apostle Paul warned that the day would come when people would "heap to themselves teachers, having itching ears" (2 Tim. 4:3). It was in that context that Paul said, "Preach the word; be instant in season, out of season; reprove, rebuke, exhort with all long-suffering and doctrine" (2 Tim. 4:2).

Preaching, at its best, is to open the eyes, prick the conscience, and stir our hearts toward God. If we know what is good for us we will get back to the basics. We will stop preaching a watered-down gospel to a washed-out generation. We will stop giving six easy steps on how to keep joy in your life to people who know that life is not easy. We will return to preaching the narrow way.

A layman expressed the longings of many when he recently said to me, and he was not wanting to be critical of his pastor, "I don't care much for those clever little sermon series. I want my pastor to get a message from God each week. And when I go to church I need a sermon, not a psychological talk."

Helmut Thielicke tells of walking along a city street in Hamburg, Germany, about the time in the morning when your breakfast is but a memory and lunch time is two hours away. He saw a sign on an establishment. It read, "FRESH BREAD FOR SALE."

Just like Pavlov's dog, his mouth began to water, his stomach to growl and his mind said, "Why not? One piece of fresh bread, warm from the baker's oven, won't mess up your lunch too much." He entered the building and asked for a slice of bread. The clerk smiled and said, "Sir, I'm sorry. We don't make bread. We make signs."

It would be tragic if some hungry soul, some spiritually starved person came to your church only to discover that you are better at marketing the church than preaching the gospel, that we don't produce what we promise.

De-Ice the Hymnal Covers

Second only to the preaching of God's word, and a close second at that, is the place of music in worship. What I believe about music in worship is built on four premises:

- There are no great churches without great music.
- There is no great music without great congregational singing.
- There is no great congregational singing unless men sing.

  (Women usually sing more readily than men.)

- Neither men nor women will sing unless the music is heart music.

A smaller church with a limited staff and limited talent would do best to focus on congregational singing. If you can lead the congregation to sing, you can have a great worship service even if you don't have the greatest soloists and the greatest musical talent.

Some churches have great choir programs but they do not have great worship services because they are geared to performance rather than congregational participation. The Bible is not silent on music in worship. The apostle Paul said, "Let the word of Christ dwell in you richly in all wisdom; teaching and admonishing one another in psalms and hymns and spiritual songs, singing with grace in your hearts to the Lord" (Col. 3:16).

And again he writes, "Speaking to yourselves in psalms and hymns and spiritual song, singing and making melody in your heart to the Lord" (Eph. 5:19).

Great choirs and soloists are not necessary to do any of that. In fact, special music is a relatively recent innovation in worship. B. H. Carroll, longtime pastor of First Baptist Church of Waco and founder of Southwestern Seminary, believed that the sole purpose of the church choir was to lead and unify the congregational singing and for the choir to sing by itself "is worse than an absurdity. It is a sin when habitual."

We may, in time, if things continue, discover he was right. It is for sure better not to have specials than for them to be poorly done.

So, major on congregational singing. A good pianist and a good congregational song leader can awaken any

worship service. But keep in mind, most men will not respond to music unless it is easy to sing and has the kind of
melody a person might hum as he goes about his work.

I was interim pastor at a church once where the music
was so high we had to de-ice the hymnal covers before we
took off lest we crash in mid-chorus. After a few weeks I
requested that we sing more familiar hymns, like "Amazing Grace," "When We All Get To Heaven," "How Great
Thou Art," and "Love Lifted Me."

In the weeks that followed I received 40 to 50 letters,
all but two of them from men, thanking me for changing
the music program. The first letter I received was a thank
you note from a banker who wrote, "Yesterday's music
kept me humming all day — in fact I came into work
whistling our music this morning."

Unless you are singing the kind of music that people
can hum and whistle while they work, I can assure you
you are missing the congregation. And if the people do
not sing, then the service will be dull and dead.

That kind of music may not challenge the choir, but
the purpose of church music is not to challenge the choir.
It is to worship God. For that to happen the congregation
must participate.

God's House — A House of Prayer

Third, prayer has to be an important part of meaningful
worship. Prayer is our personal link with God. Without
prayer there is no personal and dynamic relationship with
God and there can be no vitality in worship. Jesus taught us
that when he cleansed the temple of the money changers.

In his day the house of God had been turned into a

place of merchandise. Worshippers were being gouged by the merchants who sold animals at highly inflated prices to be used in sacrifices and there was so much haggling over prices that the temple was too noisy for a worshipper to think, much less pray. Jesus, seeing this, turned over the money changers' tables and drove those who sold animals out of the house of God saying, "My house shall be called the house of prayer" (Matt. 21:13).

Do we really believe that the purpose of worship is to meet God? Do we really believe we meet God in prayer? Do we really believe that God's house is the place of prayer? If so, then silence and prayer need to have a greater place in worship.

By the way, this experience alone causes me to wonder if God is really interested in all the noise of our contemporary clamoring in worship, even if it does draw a crowd. We may need to hear again the admonition of the Lord through the psalmist, "Be still and know that I am God" (Ps. 46:10).

Pass the Collection Plate, Please

Finally, giving has always been a part of true worship. Abraham, long before God commanded us to do so, gave tithes of all he possessed to Melchizedek, the priest of God (Gen. 14:18). He did it not because he had to do it, but because he wanted to give. It was apparently a voluntary expression of his gratitude to God for his goodness and grace.

Jacob, without coercion or command, after a night of wrestling with God, made a vow to God, "If God will be with me, and keep me in the way that I am going, and will give me bread to eat and clothing to put on, so that I come back to my father's house in peace, then the Lord shall be my God... and all that you give me I will surely give a tenth to you" (Gen. 28:20-22). He did it not out of obligation, but out of adoration and appreciation.

It was under Moses that tithing became a sacred duty. "And all the tithes of the land, whether of the sea or the land, or of the fruit of the tree, is the Lord's: it is holy unto the Lord" (Lev. 27:30).

In the New Testament neither our Savior nor his apostles commanded tithing, but Jesus did endorse it (Matt. 23:23). This affirmation alone suggests that tithing is a vital part of worship.

Giving, then, is not just a means of paying the bills. It is a way of making a spiritual sacrifice to God (Heb. 13:15-16).

The offering, then, is a solemn act of worship. My boyhood pastor, John M. Wright, made an indelible impression on me when every Sunday, before the offering was taken, he opened the scriptures and read, "Upon the first day of the week, let everyone of you lay by him in store, as God has prospered him, that there be no gatherings when I come" (I Cor. 16:2).

That set the tone for the offering as an act of worship, not a means of raising the church budget or paying the church bills.

Pastor, wake up the worship! Make it dynamic, interesting, and alive without using shallow emotion or cheap entertainment. Depth, dignity, and devotion should characterize worship at its best.

For years I have said, "You build the spirit of the church through the worship service and you grow the church through an effective Sunday School." So, pastor, pay attention to worship. It's the way to wake up a sleeping congregation.

Chapter 5

How to Awaken a Sleeping Church Without Disturbing It

I heard a new definition of insanity recently. It is to keep doing the same things over and over again and expect different results. Unfortunately, that's the story of many smaller churches today. To visit them is often like stepping into a time machine that takes you back to the 1950s. Their facilities, their order of services, their structure, their programs, their methods are virtually the same as they were in those "glory days" of Southern Baptists. Is it any wonder so many of our churches have plateaued or are in decline?

If our churches are to come alive, be dynamic and vital again, they must make some changes. It doesn't make sense to think we can keep doing the same things in the same way year after year and things not to be the same.

That, however, is where the rub comes in. A pastor must not try to change too much too soon. You must not get too far ahead of your people. You must remain sensitive to them and carry them with you or you will lose your leadership and your opportunity to do anything at all. You must walk that fine line between idealism and realism.

There are several reasons why change comes slow to smaller and older churches. First, people are naturally resistant to change. Even I don't like change except that which I initiate. Older people are especially that way. And a smaller church is likely to have a large number of older people in its membership.

In addition, a smaller church is likely to have a close-knit power structure comprised of two or three families who virtually run the church. In one of my early pastorates the chairman of the deacons had held that position for over 20 years. His brother was also a deacon, as was his son-in-law and his son-in-law's father. In that smaller church the vote of these men and their families alone was enough to determine the outcome of most issues that came before the church. In similar power structures these parties often are little thinkers; that's why the church has remained small. That was definitely not the case in the church I pastored, but nonetheless, in any church, it's the little thinkers who are the big stinkers.

And again, some churches are reluctant to change because, as I have already suggested, they have seen pastors come and go with great regularity. A new pastor often introduces change and about the time he has everyone and everything upset, he moves on. And as soon as he is gone, things reverted right back to the way they were done before. After seeing that process repeated several times, who wouldn't be gun-shy of change? So, go slow with proposed changes. Give the people time to think and to talk, to accept your ideas, and to accept you.

Try not to force a showdown between yourself and the leadership of the church if at all possible. Remember, the people in a smaller church have lived, worked, and worshipped together for years. Many of them are related. They plan to continue to live there the rest of their lives. They don't expect you to. So, if there's a showdown, don't expect them to side with you against their friends, neighbors, customers, and family. If they have to choose, you'll lose.

The fellowship of a church is fragile. It can be divided quicker and more deeply over a pastor than anyone or anything else (1 Cor. 1-2). The wise and discerning pastor will not let the people be divided over him or some issue he may propose. It is better to back off than to break up the church.

The real question that confronts the pastor of every smaller church is how to awaken a sleeping church without disturbing it, i.e., without angering and alienating the people. He must figure out how to get the church on the cutting edge without being on the bleeding edge.

It's a given, if you keep doing what you've always done, you will keep getting what you've always gotten. Change, then, is essential to progress. So, how do we change things to take the church forward? That's the real issue.

There are lots of things a pastor can do to awaken a sleeping church that people can't argue about, that won't create dissension, that don't require a vote. Those are the places to start. Let me suggest seven things you can do to awaken a sleeping church without disturbing it:

- Do things people can see and will be proud of.
- Do things people don't have to vote on.
- Do things people will enjoy.
- Do things people have done before at other times or in other places.
- Do things that honor the people.
- Do things that involve the people.
- Do things that will encourage the people.

Make Them Proud

First, you can do some things that the people can see and will be proud of. A good place to start is by shaping up the buildings and grounds. This is one of the quickest ways to show that change and progress are taking place in the church. And this can usually be done without a great deal of dissension or discussion.

In my last pastorate we adopted a small, established, declining church in our community as a mission. The church building had been erected in the 1950s and had all the characteristics of a church from that era. The entrance to the church had two iron oil field pipes as posts for the porch, a small steeple atop the sanctuary that was out of proportion to the size of the building, and the style of brick sign in the front that clearly identified the era in which it was erected.

One of the first things we did was to give the new pastor, Matthew McKeller, $10,000 from our local mission fund and encouraged him to fix up the outside of the building. He replaced the old steeple with a new fiberglass one that was in right proportion for the building. He needed an architect to help him determine that. He replaced the steel pipes with attractive colonial columns. He put up a modern sign. And he landscaped the grounds. Those things changed the outward appearance of the building. In a few weeks the facilities were transformed from a 1950's look to an up-to-date appearance. The people took pride in what they saw and were soon ready to do renovations on the inside of the buildings to match the attractive outside. The remodeling of the church instilled a sense of pride and satisfaction in the people and started the church moving. With new leadership and a new spirit, that church that had declined to 20 in Sunday School attendance is now averaging over 300.

The custodians at my church always understood the grounds were to be manicured. I wanted grass everywhere grass was supposed to be. And I didn't want grass anywhere grass was not supposed to be. There was to be no grass between the cracks in the sidewalks, between the curb and the streets, or in the flower beds. The shrubs were to be trimmed and the grass to be mowed every week. The entrances to the church were to be swept before services every Sunday. The buildings were to be kept painted. I believe that God's house ought to be the best kept building in the community. The people caught this sense of pride and they not only appreciated it, it became a part of their thinking.

You probably can do something similar to that where you serve. Why not paint the building inside and out? Replace old and worn out carpet? Put cushions on the pews? Improve the lighting system? Landscape the grounds? Put up a new sign?

If the general church budget is tight, encourage people to give money for these projects in memory of a loved one. In addition to honoring people, this can get the job done.

Well-kept buildings and grounds send a silent message. It says, "There is someone around here who cares." It sends a visual message to the church membership and the community alike about the pride and class of the church. And, believe me, that can make a big difference.

No Vote Is Necessary

Second, do things that don't have to be voted on and that no one can oppose. Call the people to prayer. That's undoubtedly the best place to begin if you want to see real change in the church. The late Dr. Abner McCall told that when he was president of Baylor University five students came to him one day and wanted him to proclaim a revival meeting. They wanted to get a tent, enlist an evangelist, and conduct a revival meeting on campus. He said to them, "That's not the way it works. What you need to do is to start praying for revival. In fact," he said, "let's become the first prayer group of five. Then after we have prayed a while, let's organize another group of five and another and another and another. God will begin to work. When God works then we'll get the tent and the evangelist."

That was good advice to them and to us. God has chosen to work in response to his people's prayers. But do we really believe in the power of prayer? A man got a permit to open the first tavern in a small town. The members of the local church were strongly opposed to the bar, so they began to pray that God would intervene. A few days before the tavern was scheduled to open, lightning hit the structure and it burned to the ground.

The people in the church were surprised, but pleased. But then they received notice that the tavern owner was suing them. He declared that their prayers were responsible for the burning of the building. They denied the charge.

At the end of the preliminary hearing, the judge summarized the situation succinctly: "It seems that the tavern owner believes in the power of prayer and the church people don't!"

William Carey's sister was disabled and unable to walk. Yet, she felt called to the mission field just as much as her brother. But, because of her handicap she could not go. She said on one occasion, "I cannot go to India on my feet, but I can go to India on my knees." We can go lots of places on our knees we could never go to on our feet.

It is prayer, more than anything else, that changes churches and people. Hudson Taylor said, "It's possible to move men to God through prayer alone." But it isn't quick and easy prayer. It is disciplined, dedicated, persistent prayer. So if you want to change the church, call the people to prayer. Nobody can argue with that.

Start a discipleship group. Select two or three, five or six, people or couples and invest a good part of your life in them. Hand pick them. That's what Jesus did. He never asked for volunteers. He enlisted his disciples.

Meet them for Bible study and prayer once a week. You can meet in your home, in their home, or at a local restaurant. You can meet for breakfast, lunch, or dinner, depending on their availability.

Spend time with them. Go hunting and fishing and

golfing with your men. Jesus chose the 12 that they might be with him. He taught them not just in formal sessions but as they traveled along the way.

Through informal times, church members will catch your spirit and will learn from you. What better could you do to change your church than to invest two or three years of your life in the lives of some of your key people who have great potential and who will still be in the church long after you are gone? And nobody can be upset at your having breakfast with some members for Bible study and prayer.

Start a jail ministry. Ask the local sheriff if you can hold services in the jail on Sunday afternoons. Take a few laymen with you. If someone plays the guitar, let him lead the group in singing "Amazing Grace," "When We All Get to Heaven," or other familiar hymns. Then share your testimony and bring a brief gospel message. In time, give the responsibility for the testimony and message to the laymen. Not many people would oppose that.

I began a jail ministry in three churches, and I did get one negative reaction. When I announced the first service, the banker's wife said in astonishment, "I can't believe our church is going to the jail to preach." She thought it was beneath our dignity. Then I reminded her of Jesus' words, "I was in jail and ye came unto me" (Matt. 25:36). And that was the end of that.

One of my deacons who regularly participated in this ministry said to me years later, "Before you came as pastor I did not know how to share my faith effectively. But after sharing it at the jail all these years, I can now witness to anyone, anywhere, anytime." Needless to say, the jail ministry changed his life and had a measurable effect on the church.

Start a nursing home ministry. Contact the director of the local nursing home and ask if your church can conduct Sunday afternoon worship services. If services are not already being conducted there, the people will welcome you. The nurses and directors will be happy to gather the people in a central meeting room. You can purchase an electronic keyboard at a nominal price. Get someone to lead the people in familiar hymns. Let the people make requests. You lead the first few services, then ask different Sunday School classes to be in charge on different Sundays. This can involve all age groups, even the children, in a meaningful ministry.

Begin a visitation night. Set a night and lead the people in visiting the lost, unenlisted, and backslidden in your community. If it's a small community the people may have a difficult time going to visit friends and neighbors they have known all of their life . . . and perhaps witnessed to before. Use good judgment on how hard you press this issue. If men have been visiting with one another at the general store or the fire station for years, it will be extremely difficult for them to suddenly begin calling on these people for the church. Be sensitive and understanding as to how much you push this. But no one can really oppose these kinds of things.

You Go Forward By Going Backward

Third, do things people have done before — either in other places or in other days. Put up a tent and conduct an outside revival meeting. The tent can be rented, often through your state evangelism department, shipped in by freight truck, and easily erected by your men. The tent alone will be the best publicity you can have in a small town.

In Taylor, the high school was located across the street from the church. I secured permission to put up a tent and we conducted an outside revival meeting there. The elderly and infirm could park adjacent to the tent and listen to the services with their car windows rolled down. The people dressed informally. People came to that revival meeting who seldom darkened the doors of any church. It was the best revival we had in the five years I was pastor there.

Tent revivals are a throwback to days gone by. But the church had not had one in so long it was a novelty. It is often easier to go back to something that has been done before than to do something the people have never heard of.

Baptize outside if there is a river or lake nearby. In San Marcos we moved our Sunday evening services outside every Sunday night in August. I baptized in the San Marcos River which ran through the city park. We sat on the river bank in lawn chairs and on quilts. We set up an outside public address system, and people came dressed casually. The baptism and outside services attracted many visitors. The service was followed by homemade ice cream and watermelon socials.

Sometimes it is easier to go backward than it is to go forward. And, some of these old things are actually so old that they become new. Getting a church going is much like getting a car out of the mud. Once it's stuck, you sometimes have to roll it back before you can get it to move forward. Churches can be the same way.

Have a Good Time

Fourth, do things the people will enjoy. Have an all-church picnic some Sunday afternoon at a park or at a local lake. Have games and contests. Set up a portable PA system for worship. Let the people bring lawn chairs or blankets to sit on. The people will enjoy it.

Have a homecoming. Let it commemorate the founding of the church. Honor the charter members of the congregation. Invite people to come back and celebrate with you. It will be a happy time.

Have a revival and invite former pastors back to preach each night. Each one of them is the favorite preacher of some members of the congregation. Each of these pastors married certain people, buried certain people, and baptized certain people in the congregation. They will have special ties to different people. The people will rejoice at seeing them again and hearing them again. And, by the way, always speak well of former pastors and welcome them back. It will endear you to the people and be an example of Christian grace. There is no need for jealousy or competition in God's work. And there is enough room in people's hearts to love several ministers at the same time.

Erect a basketball goal or build a volleyball court and have Friday night recreation for youth or young couples. Encourage them to invite their friends who do not attend church. Be there yourself. You will develop a good relationship with your people and establish new relationships with prospects. Many of these people never know a preacher outside the pulpit. Once they learn that you are a fun-loving, normal part of the human race, they may want to come and hear you preach. I've seen it happen many times.

Have Sunday night socials following the evening worship services. Homemade ice cream, watermelon, cake or pie and coffee will bring the people together for a good time.

When people enjoy one another, love one another, and fellowship with one another, the church comes alive. The pastor can create opportunities where such activities take place. Just don't overdo it.

Give Honor to Whom Honor Is Due

Fifth, do things that honor the people. Recognize and honor the deacons, Sunday School workers, graduating seniors, new babies and new parents. When you appreciate, honor, and recognize the people they will reciprocate. It's hard not to love and respect someone who loves and respects you.

I referred to the deacons and the power structure of the church earlier. Some pastors complain that the deacons in smaller churches run the church. Well, instead of complaining, thank God they do. If they didn't, the church would be virtually without leadership. In most smaller churches preachers come and go with such regularity that if it were not for these people, there would be no continuity of leadership in the church at all.

Honor mothers on Mother's Day. Honor servicemen on the Fourth of July. Honor teachers and students on "back to school" Sunday. Such people are worthy of honor.

Get the People Going

Sixth, do things that involve the people. Develop short term projects that the people can participate in. If it can be done in a day, all the better. Once they get a taste of one ministry they may develop an appetite for more. When I was interim pastor at the Casa View Baptist Church, Dallas, Texas, the members went throughout their community leaving a sack of corn chips and a small jar of salsa on each doorstep. With it was a note that said, "Man does not live by bread alone. He needs a little salsa now and then," and an invitation to attend the church. Those two items were a natural fit with the church's Hispanic name. Members called back later to issue a personal invitation if the people were not home.

A church in Virginia took a free light bulb to every home in their community. Attached to the bulb was a note pointing to Jesus as "the light of the world." These short term, one shot projects can often involve people in ways they would otherwise never get involved.

Lift Them Up

Finally, do things that encourage the people. Set a high attendance day. Encourage each class to reach a certain percentage of their enrollment or to have the highest attendance in their history. The cumulative effect of this will be the highest attendance in the history of the church. This can encourage a church that may have been down, discouraged and defeated for years. Anything that can be done to show progress and achievement will help encourage them.

Do some fun things that the people will enjoy, that

unite the people . . . let them see something happen. It's easier to get other things going once they see progress being made and they are proud of it.

Someone once said to D. L. Moody, "I don't like your methods." He replied, "I don't particularly like all of them either. What are yours?" The man answered, "I don't have any." Moody then replied, "Well, in that case, I like the way I'm doing it a whole lot better than the way you're not doing it."

If you've got better ideas than these, then for heaven's sake, and I do mean heaven's sake, use them. But do something. It's a matter of life and death.

Chapter 6

Discouragement: Pastoral Enemy Number One

It's hard to raise a growing family. It's harder still to care for an aging one. To take care of an elderly parent, to sit with a terminally ill patient, can be straining and draining, especially if it has been a long and painful illness with no hope of improvement. That can be as hard on the caregiver as it is on the patient.

It is the same with churches. When a church has an aging membership, when it is located in a declining area, when its best days are in the past and it is slowly dying, to be its pastor can be a strain and a drain. It can be as discouraging a work as one can be engaged in.

Recently Minnesota Twins outfielder Kirby Puckett, whose team, at that time had the worst record in the Major League, said, "There are peaks and valleys in this game. We're in a valley — Death Valley."

Death Valley is a terrible place for churches as well as teams to be. And it's a major challenge to either coach or pastor in such a place and at such a time. But that is where most churches are today.

One of the main sufferings experienced in the ministry today, especially the ministry of pastors in smaller churches, is that of low self-esteem. Increasingly, many perceive themselves as having very little impact. They are very busy, but they do not see much change. It seems that their efforts are fruitless. Is it any wonder they are discouraged?

Discouragement, of course, is not unique to pastors. It is one of the major obstacles in every Christian's life. There is a fable that the devil decided once to have an auction. He decided to go out of business and sell his tools. The auction day came, and a great crowd of people gathered. He placed all his tools out on a red plush mat. The tools were envy, jealousy, greed, avarice, vengeance, resentment, hatred — all of them.

Off to the side, he had a silver wedge. Someone asked him what it was and he said, "That's a silver wedge. See how bright and shiny it is? I use it all the time. It is the best tool I have. I put it over there because it is the most valuable. It is worth more than all the other tools put together."

They asked, "Well, how do you use it?"

Satan answered, "That's the wedge of discouragement. You take the finest Christian, one who has received Jesus Christ into his life and who is trying to serve him, and drive the wedge of discouragement into his Christian work and wreck his usefulness. I can drive that wedge in and pry open a door, and all the rest of my cohorts can go in. I can break that life down with discouragement."

It is just a fable, but it is no less true. The wedge of discouragement is the devil's most powerful tool with ministers. Judging from the mail that crosses my desk, from the phone calls I receive, and from the personal counseling I do, I'd say discouragement is pastoral enemy number one. It is something every pastor must deal with if he is to maintain an effective ministry.

Do you know what worries me most about our churches and ministers today? It is not that our young people are coming out of our seminaries cross-threaded theologically. What worries me most is that many of those who have been in the ministry five, ten, twenty years have lost their song. They're just muddling along — no fire, no excitement, no joy, no hope. They are not using their pastoral gifts to the fullest. They are discouraged and defeated.

If we are going to win our world to Christ and change our churches, we won't do it with disheartened, defeated pastors. We must recapture our enthusiasm. We must recover our song.

Paul's admonition to Timothy is apropos for us when he wrote, "Stir up the gift of God which is within you" (2 Tim. 1:6). The word "stir" in the original language means "to fan again to flames." In this statement the apostle Paul pictures Timothy's pastoral gift as a fire that once blazed brightly, but had gone out. Underneath the dull, gray ashes there were still hot coals, capable of bursting into flames again, if they were just stirred up, if they were fanned.

We don't know what happened to put the fire out in

Timothy's life. Maybe it was persecution. Maybe it was criticism. Maybe people had thrown cold water on too many of his ideas. Maybe he had just grown weary in well doing. Whatever it was, something had happened and the fire had gone out. Paul knew Timothy would never reach his maximum for Christ unless he caught fire again. Hence the counsel, "fan again to flames the gift of God that is within thee."

Pastoral leaders need that same challenge today. There are three things the pastor of a smaller church can do to rekindle his enthusiasm and avoid discouragement. He can:

- Remember the law of the harvest.
- Use the right standard to evaluate his work.
- Trust in God.

Output and Outcome

First, to avoid discouragement, a pastor needs to re-member the law of the harvest. The apostle Paul once wrote, as both a warning and an encouragement, "Let us not be weary in well doing: for in due season we shall reap, if we faint not" (Gal. 6:9).

Paul had been encouraging the churches of Galatia to be generous and to do good. He realized that this was not easy to do in tough times. When the work was difficult and the opposition was stiff, when response was slow and the workers were uncooperative, it was hard to stay faith-ful and optimistic. So he reminded his friends of the law of the harvest.

The law of the harvest says if you keep planting good seed in good soil in God's good time there will be fruit. If you stay faithful, in time, you will be fruitful.

Of course, not all fields are equally productive agriculturally. Nor are they spiritually. Agriculturally, some fields are rich and fertile. The soil will grow anything that is planted in it. On the other hand, the soil of other fields has been overworked. It is worn out and depleted. When that is the case, you can plow faithfully and plant diligently and wait patiently, but the yield will be meager because of the quality of the soil.

It is the same with church fields. Some church fields are rich and fertile. They have prospects galore. Visitors attend church freely. Additions are abundant. But other church fields have been overworked and are depleted. There are few new people moving in. Those who have been there a long time are hard and calloused. In the first two communities where I pastored, every lost man around had been witnessed to a dozen times. At least once a year, during the church's fall revival meeting, the pastor would take the visiting evangelist to talk to them, especially if they were the husband of one of the faithful women in the church. These people usually knew more gospel than the preacher. And they had more excuses for not being saved than he had ever thought of. Response to the gospel is slow at best, no matter how hard you work. In such places, your fruitfulness is not necessarily an indication of your faithfulness.

I had an exceedingly fruitful ministry at Green Acres in Tyler. We averaged 13 new members per Sunday for 17 years in a row. And, our average Sunday School attendance increased more than 100 per year each of those years — from 700 to 2,500.

But, I was just as faithful and I worked just as hard, if not harder, while at the First Baptist Church, San Marcos, and the First Baptist Church, Taylor, without seeing that kind of response. What was the difference? There were many factors that played a part, not the least of which was the productivity of the different fields. In God's work, as in agriculture, it doesn't matter how hard you work, if the field is not fertile the fruit will not be abundant. From a limited and overworked field, the response will be meager.

This is not an excuse for laziness. There is enough of that in the ministry already. It is an attempt to encourage the faithful pastor who works hard but sees little results. The problem may not be you. It may be where you are. It may be your location, not your dedication.

We are to work hard no matter where we are. Sixteen times in his epistles the apostle Paul spoke of "laboring" for Christ. The word "laborer" literally means "to toil," "to exhaust yourself," "to feel fatigue." Paul worked hard for Christ, he literally wore himself out in God's work and so should we.

Bob Flegle, who directs Sunday School and Church Growth for the Northwest Baptist Convention, told of a pastor in his state whose church was in the growth spiral. He told Bob one day, "I wish this could be a whole lot more spiritual and a lot less work."

That's just the way God's work is. It is holy, but it is also hard. It is glorious, but it is also grueling. And we are to be diligent in it. There's a poem that reminds us of the dangers inherent in spiritual laziness. It is called "Sitting by the Fire":

He wasn't much for moving about
It wasn't his desire.
While others sought to build the church,
He was sitting by the fire.

Same old story, day by day,
He never seemed to tire.
No matter what the others did,
He was sitting by the fire.

At last he died, as all must do.
They say he went up higher.
But, if he's doing what he used to do,
He's sitting by the fire.

Pastors need to remember the law of the harvest. It can save us from despair in hard times. With us, as it was with the Christians at Galatia, it's hard to keep your spirits up when the work is down. Pastors sometimes feel like they're polishing brass on a sinking ship. Nobody wants to be the cruise director on the Titanic.

Above all, remember that we are responsible for the output, not the outcome. The outcome is God's business. If we are faithful in discharging our responsibilities, God will be faithful in his. If we plant, in time we will reap. So, in times of discouragement, in the dry times and the difficult times, in the times when criticism is strong, remember the law of the harvest.

Use the Right Measurements

Second, to avoid discouragement, a pastor needs to apply the right measurements of success to his ministry. Each year I sit at a desk in the Annuity Board booth at the

Southern Baptist Convention and autograph books the Board provides free of charge to the pastors who attend the convention. I ask most of these pastors the same question, "How are things going in your church?" With few exceptions the answers are quantitative: "Our membership is up 10 percent . . . 50 baptisms so far this year . . . We're starting a new building . . . We're going to two worship services . . ."

No wonder the church has an identity crisis. We are measuring it against the wrong standard. Cultural values have so captured the church that we equate success with size and growth alone. And more often than not a minister's performance is measured not by faithfulness to the gospel but by whether the people keep coming and giving.

We tend to idolize, recognize, and utilize those churches that are growing and the pastors who are leading them. If the church is not growing in number, we assume someone is doing something wrong. Either the pastor and the deacons haven't analyzed the market well enough or they haven't invested in the right program or they aren't working hard.

That's why church growth has not only become big business, it also emulates big business. And it is why it has become the hottest business in the religious world today.

Church growth may be a sign of God's blessings. It surely was when Peter preached at Pentecost. People were convicted, they repented, and were baptized — 3,000 on the first day; and the Lord "added to the church daily" (Acts 2:47), with 5,000 in one day alone (Acts 4:4). But it was the Lord adding to the numbers, not marketing experts.

But I say again, not all churches can grow numerically. If we expect them to, if we compare ourselves to others, then we are bound to feel we are failures. For sure, we are not bound to grow at any cost. Our goals and methods must be honorable and consistent with the gospel. What matters most is biblical fidelity. The measure of a church's effectiveness is spiritual, not numerical growth.

What is a worthy goal for a church? It's not just to build a big church. That can be the worst kind of self seeking. The fact is, the whole church growth movement has some dangers inherent in it. One is that we shall be more concerned about building our own kingdom than we are in building his. When I was a pastor I had to ask myself on a regular basis, "Whose kingdom am I trying to build, his or mine?" And I didn't always like the answer. Beware! Church growth can be very self serving.

Stephen Arterburn and Jack Felton have written a book titled *Toxic Faith: Understanding and Overcoming Religious Addiction.* They warn, "Faith becomes toxic when individuals use God or religion for profit, power, pleasure, or prestige." It does happen.

So, what is a worthy goal for a church? It is this — to get the maximum yield from your field. The Lord has put you in a particular place at a particular time. Your job is to work the field to get the maximum production from it for him.

Don't compare yourself to or measure yourself by others. That can only lead to a sense of pride if you do better than they, or envy, jealousy, and despair if you do worse. What you need to do is to analyze your situation. You need to look at your own potential. Figure out how to reach it and go after it. You are only obligated to do the best you can where you are for Jesus' sake today.

If your church is located in an older, established neighborhood, then significant growth is unlikely. You must assume in such a place or a declining rural area that everyone who wants to attend church is already going. Those who don't attend church have said by their actions, "We don't want to go." That's a tough crowd to reach. Some of them can be reached and we should make every effort to do so, but it is slow and difficult work. You might be able to attract them by a side show, or a circus and carnival atmosphere, but it won't be lasting growth. The fact is, about the only churches where significant numerical growth is taking place are new churches in growing neighborhoods.

So, what are some legitimate growth measurements other than total membership? Try these:

- Percentage of resident membership in regular Bible study
- Percentage of resident members making financial contributions
- Per-capita gifts to the church
- Percentage of contributors pledging to tithe
- Percentage of resident members accepting an assigned, accountable duty
- Percentage of the church budget going to missions
- Number of contacts made with shut-ins
- Number of examples of creative ministry in the community
- Number of children enrolled for Vacation Bible School
- Reduction of church debt
- Growth of endowment for the church cemetery or other purposes

- Systematic upkeep and improvement in church property
- Number of new teachers, leaders trained
- Number of young people answering God's call to vocational Christian service
- Number of children graduating from high school
- Number of children going to college

Don't forget to regularly congratulate your people for their growth. Help them find ways to celebrate the life of the church. Call attention to examples of love and ministry. Even if you thought of the idea, give credit to the people who made it happen.

God Is Still God

Finally, to avoid discouragement, a pastor needs to keep trusting the Lord. In a time when the foundations are crumbling, it's awfully easy to be despondent. What can we do? We wonder if there is any hope. G. K. Chesterton said, "At least five times in the twentieth century the faith has, to all appearances, gone to the dogs. But in each of those five cases it was the dog that died." Our crumbling beliefs and our denominational decline do not diminish God.

When the Japanese invaded Yangcheng more than 50 years ago, Gladys Aylward, missionary to China, was forced to flee. But she couldn't leave her work behind. With only one assistant, she led more than 100 orphans over the mountains toward free China. During the harrowing journey out of war-torn Yangcheng she grappled with despair as never before. After passing a sleepless night, she faced the morning with no hope of reaching safety. A 13-year-old girl in the group reminded her of their much-loved story of Moses and the Israelites crossing the Red Sea.

"But I'm not Moses," Gladys cried in desperation.

"Of course, you aren't," the girl said, "but Jehovah is still God."

We need to remember who we are. But we also need to remember who he is. It can help save us from our greatest enemy — discouragement.

We are not the first generation of church leaders to face discouraging times. In the summer of 1865 James P. Boyce and John A. Broadus met with the faculty of Southern Seminary to consider resuming classes. They had been suspended because of the Civil War. The outlook was bleak. The students were few. The resources were meager. After a lengthy discussion, John Broadus rose to say, "Suppose we quietly agree that this seminary may die, but we'll die first."

That's the kind of resolve and commitment we need to do God's work today. Pastoring is not for the weak, the timid or the hesitant. It's tough, demanding, and often discouraging work. Let's you and I quietly agree, our work may die, but we will not give up in despair. We will die first.

Chapter 7

Pitfalls to the Pastorate

During the 1992 Dallas Cowboy training camp, Nate Newton was discussing one of Jimmy Johnson's favorite tenets. He said, "It's not the good plays that win the game. It's the bad plays that lose it."

That is true not only in professional football, but it is also true in life and the ministry. You can spend a lifetime doing good and blow everything with one bad play. As the Japanese proverb says, "The reputation of a thousand years may be determined by the conduct of one hour."

There are lots of people who tell us what can ruin our lives and spoil our ministry. One minister named four things that all start with "s" — sloth, silver, sex, and self.

Harry Truman said, "There are three things on this earth that will ruin a man — power, money, and women. If a man can accept power as a temporary thing, he's going to be all right. But if he thinks he's the cause of the power, that will ruin him. And money, if a man makes too much money, too quickly, it can separate him from the rest of the human race who have to work most of their lives just to earn a living. And if a man is disloyal to his family, that will ruin him. 'Cause if you've got the right partner in life, you're not going to have much trouble."

I drove from Dallas to Dennison, Texas, early one Sunday morning several years ago to preach at First Baptist Church. I arrived early, so I stopped at a small cafe to get a cup of coffee. The jukebox was playing a country and western song that captured my attention. It was titled, "Savior, Save Us From Ourselves."

We are often our own worst enemy in the ministry. With that in mind, let me share with you some pitfalls to the pastorate that we need to be aware of, some things we need to be saved from. There are six of them:

- Indiscretion with women
- Mismanagement of money
- Unwieldy ambition
- Inability to get along with people
- Pride
- Professionalism

We Are Never Home Free

One pitfall to the pastorate is sexual misconduct. The Bible records numerous accounts of God's servants who failed through sexual sins. It is still one of the most common causes of failure in the ministry. In a survey of clergy conducted by *Leadership*, a publication owned by *Christianity Today*, almost one in four clergy admitted engaging in inappropriate sexual conduct. According to the Baptist Sunday School Board it is the second most common reason for firing among Southern Baptist clergy.

I talked recently with Jack Kelly, senior vice president of commercial marketing for Preferred Risk Mutual Insurance Company, a company that provides property and casualty insurance for more than 6,000 Southern Baptist churches. He told me that they deal with at least one lawsuit a week of a church being sued for sexual misconduct. Thankfully, not all these are Southern Baptist churches. Who knows how many other cases are just swept under the rug?

The lure to unfaithfulness is perhaps greater for the pastor than even for the average person. Tony Campolo warns that, "In a very real sense, the nature of being a church leader is to become a sex object. It is very naive to assume that the only thing that turns people on is good looks. The truth is that power, influence, and prestige have tremendous capacity to stimulate sexual excitement. Church leaders often find themselves unwittingly eliciting powerful sexual response."

We must constantly be on guard against the temptations of the flesh. The romantic impulse never dies in us. When God saves us he doesn't drain the red blood out of our veins and fill them with buttermilk. If a spark falls on a block of ice nothing happens. But if it falls on something combustible, there is the possibility of a raging fire. It is the same with our emotions. We are never home free. Jerome, who translated the Latin Vulgate, and who spent years of his life in a monastery, said that there still lingered in his mind visions of dancing girls.

There is never an excuse for exploiting for personal gratification the power and privilege of pastoral relationship. But it does happen. The evidence shows that most ministers who succumb to sexual temptation are not seeking an extramarital affair, but at least they give it permission to happen. Such permission should never be given.

Nothing can guarantee that you can successfully avoid temptation, but there are some things you can do that will work significantly in your favor.

- Don't overmatch yourself. The attention of an attractive woman is always pleasant to a man and the best of people sometimes do the worst of things. We are capable of anything.

- Minimize the risk. Never counsel a woman alone. Try to have your secretary in the outer office when counseling.

- Restrict your counseling to one or two sessions at the most, and never for longer than one hour in duration. If a woman needs more counseling than this, you probably need to refer her to a professional. It's usually the prolonged counseling sessions that get ministers into trouble.

- Keep your own marriage in good repair. It is no surprise that life in the parsonage has its own stresses; and the taller the steeple the greater those can become. The grass doesn't always look greener on the other side of the fence when you water the lawn at home.

- Don't put your hands on the women you counsel. Even an innocent hug about the shoulder can be misinterpreted as affection. Avoid even holding hands while you are praying.

- Keep your spiritual resistance high. Spend ample time nurturing your spirit through prayer and Bible study. Have a healthy relationship with the Lord.

Bruce Larson tells of an old priest who was asked by a young man, "Father, when will I cease to be bothered by the sins of the flesh?"

"I wouldn't trust myself, son, until I was dead three days," the priest responded.

Watch for these warning lights:

- Finding you look forward to someone's visit — thinking, what shall I wear today? Will she like this?

- Rearranging your schedule to accommodate a certain appointment that you enjoy.

- Meeting in less-than-standard locations — lunch, her home, and so on.

- Nurturing fantasy. When pastors fall, the fall is never sudden, only the discovery. Their fall is the fault of wrong thinking well in advance of the discovery.

- Being secretive with your spouse about what's happening.

Robert Murray McCheyne (1813-1843) wrote to Daniel Edwards, who was to be a missionary to Germany. He said, "My dear friend: I know you will apply yourself to learn German; but do not forget the culture of the inner man — I mean of the heart. How diligently the cavalry officer keeps his saber clean and sharp; every stain he rubs off with the greatest care. Remember you are God's sword

— his instrument — I trust a chosen vessel unto him to bear his name. In great measure, according to the purity and perfection of the instrument, will be the success. It is not the great talents God blesses so much as great likeness to Jesus. A holy minister is an awful weapon in the hand of God."

Remember the words of the late Fred Swank, "It's okay to love all women in general, but not one in particular." For the spiritual leader, sexual sin means nothing less than the professional death penalty.

Money Can Cost You

A second pitfall to the pastorate can be the mismanagement of money. George Allen built the Washington Redskins into an NFL power and they became the Dallas Cowboys' greatest rival in the early 1970s. He spent money so freely that Redskin owner, Edward Bennett Williams, said, "I gave George an unlimited expense account, and he exceeded it."

Some preachers have the same problem. They have never learned to live within their income. That was Luther Rice's problem. He was one of our first Baptist missionaries. He and Adoniram Judson had been appointed as missionaries to India by the Congregationalists. Each traveled to India on a separate ship. Knowing they would encounter William Carey, the Baptist missionary, in India, they began to study the New Testament to substantiate their views on baptism.

Through a study of the scriptures alone, each man became convinced on his own that Baptists were right and that he should be immersed. Upon landing in India they sought out Carey and asked that he baptize them. They were now Baptist missionaries with no support base at home. Judson agreed to stay in India and Rice returned to the United States to organize Baptists into a missionary convention.

Rice did a great work but he had one glaring weakness in his life. Biographers expressed it succinctly, "He never learned to whittle his dreams down to funds available. He joined others in making debts and assuming obligations in faith that increased support would come. He was a man about whom a contemporary said, 'He had great weakness. One was excessive hopefulness.'"

Many a pastor has had trouble piled on top of trouble for the same reason — he doesn't live on available income. He has excessive hopefulness.

Through the years, ministers have gained a reputation for being notoriously poor credit risks. I heard a banker describe the three "P's" — painters, plumbers, and preachers. These are people to whom he said you should never loan money.

It is really no laughing matter when the pastor becomes a poor credit risk or when he fails to manage adequately the resources given to the church. The minister who is going to be successful must be able to manage both his money and the church's money as well.

John Wesley lived by the philosophy, "Make all you can and save all you can so you can give all you can." Charlie Shedd's financial advice was, "Give 10 percent, save 10 percent, and spend the rest with thanksgiving and joy." Both are good counsel for a pastor.

Religious Embalming Hall

The third pitfall to the pastorate is unholy ambition. Shakespeare put in the mouth of Cardinal Wolsey this warning, "Beware of ambition, for by it the angels fell."

In a day when many religious leaders have egos the size of the Goodyear blimp, when we're told that "bigger is better," in a day of show-biz religion, we must guard against the temptation of building a ministry around ourselves and not around the Lord.

None of us is ever completely immune from the desire to promote ourselves. In the television mini-series, "Peter the Great," a government leader reproved the patriarch of the Russian Orthodox Church for foolishly endorsing Peter's sinister sister as the ruler of Russia. He said, "Surely, Holy Father, you are not so close to God that you are unaware of the lusts of men."

There's nothing wrong with a pastor's quest for excellence, aggressive leadership, or the use of promotional skills. But our ego must be kept in check. It must always be subordinate to a consuming concern for the kingdom of God.

There is an old saying, "Whom the gods would curse, they call promising." Like Icarus, the mythological Greek who soared too close to the sun on wings made of wax, the pastor who tries to fly too high will soon find his wings starting to melt.

Morris Udall may have been right when he said, "The only cure for political ambition is embalming fluid." I'm sure he was right when it comes to religious ambition.

The words of Jeremiah to Baruch are good for us. "And seekest thou great things for thyself? Seek them not" (Jer. 45:5). We should, rather, seek ". . . first the kingdom of God and his righteousness; and all these other things will be added unto you" (Matt. 6:33).

Love Them Anyway

A fourth pitfall to the pastorate is the inability to get along with people. Few things will be more important in determining your success or failure than this. Honey "Fitz" Fitzpatrick, grandfather of John F. Kennedy, was asked by a reporter what was the secret to politics. He said, "Caring about people. They'll forget everything else, but they won't forget that."

It's not always easy to get along with people. Jesus did not get along with everyone. It may be hard to love people, but do it anyway. That's a part of the price of being a good pastor in a smaller church.

Someone has said it well:

People are unreasonable, illogical, and self centered.
   Love them anyway.
If you do good, people will accuse you of selfish ulterior motives.
   Do good anyway.
If you are successful, you will win false friends and true enemies.
   Succeed anyway.
Honesty and frankness make you vulnerable.
   Be honest and frank anyway.
The good you do today will be forgotten tomorrow.
   Do good anyway.

> *The biggest people with the biggest ideas can be shot down by the smallest people with the smallest minds.*
>> *Think big anyway.*
>
> *People favor underdogs but follow only top dogs.*
>> *Fight for some underdogs anyway.*
>
> *What you spend years building may be destroyed overnight.*
>> *Build anyway.*
>
> *Give the world the best you have and you'll get kicked in the teeth.*
>> *Give the world the best you've got anyway.*

In Matthew 12:18-21 there is a beautiful characterization of Jesus. It is a quotation from the prophet Isaiah that depicts the tenderness and compassion of the Messiah: "He shall not strive, nor cry; neither shall any man hear his voice in the streets. A bruised reed shall he not break, and smoking flax shall he not quench" (vv 19-20).

The word "cry" is the translation of a Greek word for a barking dog or a brawling drunken man. Jesus was not a striving, contentious man. And Jesus was not a yapper.

To the contrary, he was kind and gentle. If you are to be like him, then don't be a brawler. Remember you are a shepherd, not a yapping sheep dog.

Above all, be careful who you alienate. B. B. Crim, the old-time evangelist, made the mistake once of accepting the call of a church to be their pastor. After he had been there about six months he decided that half the church members were unsaved and led the church to turn them out. He confessed later that after he had stayed six months longer he realized he had turned the wrong half out.

Recently I was walking through the cemetery at St. John's Episcopal Church in Richmond, Virginia. It is the oldest church in Richmond, founded in 1741. It was the church where Patrick Henry gave his fiery speech, "Give me liberty or give me death."

The oldest grave in the cemetery was that of Robert Rose, the first rector of the church, who died in 1751. His epitaph read, "In his friendship he was warm and steady. In his manner he was gentle and easy; in his conversation he was entertaining and instructive. With the most tender pity he discharged all the domestic duties of husband, father, son, and brother. In short, he was a friend to the whole human race and upon that principle, a strenuous asserter and defender of liberty." That's what I'd like to be said of me. How about you?

Whose Bid Is It?

A fifth pitfall to pastors is pride. Navy chaplain Newell D. Linder tells of a sobering experience at the beginning of his ministry. "My first church was a small country mission. Full of enthusiasm and eager to build up the congregation, I decided that my sermons would set a standard of excellence heretofore unknown in the community. With high hopes I set to work."

"As I ascended the pulpit on Sunday, Paul on Mars Hill seemed sorry by comparison. The sermon was a masterpiece. The comments of the congregation at the conclusion of the service merely reaffirmed what I already knew — I was terrific! The last parishioner to leave was a lady of great age."

"'Did anyone ever tell you how wonderful you are?' she asked softly. My answer of, 'No,' lacked all vestige of conviction."

"'Well, then,' she said, 'where did you ever get the idea?'"

It's easy, with all the adulation he receives, for a preacher to get the wrong idea about himself. Dag Hammarskjöld, in his book, *Markings*, wrote, "Around a man who has been pushed into the limelight, a legend begins to grow as it does around a dead man. But a dead man is in no danger of yielding to the temptation to nourish his legend, or accept its picture as reality. I pity the man who falls in love with his image as it is drawn by public opinion during the honeymoon of publicity."

Don't get overly impressed with yourself. The church I pastored in Tyler was one of the largest in America. In addition, we had a vast television audience that covered our entire region of the state. But I often reminded myself what I imagined would happen if a group of ladies were playing bridge one day and word came to them that I had suddenly died. My guess was that one of them would say, "Oh, what a shame. He was such a nice man . . . whose bid is it?"

It's amazing today to see the number of preachers who are taking ego trips with so little luggage. At the height of his popularity, TV evangelist Robert Tilton did exactly that. He publicly proclaimed himself "the apple of God's eye." But after an exposé by CBS' *Prime Time*, his television audience began to decline, revenues plummeted, and litigation escalated. Apparently, the apple had a worm in it. He would have done well to have heeded the advice of John

Gary, a retired minister and member of one of my congregations, who said, "Stay humble so you don't stumble."

A Non-Prophet Organization

A final pitfall to the pastorate is professionalism, i.e., that our ministry will become just a job and not a passion. When that happens the church loses its prophetic voice. Unfortunately, the prophetic ministry is fast disappearing from the church today as prophets become priests. As Vance Havner put it, "The modern church is a non-prophet organization."

Then he added, "I would say to preachers, 'Beware of the disarming effect of too much familiarity with, and too many favors from, your congregation. Many a prophet is silenced by the kindness of his people. Popularity has killed more prophets than persecution.'"

Philips Brooks warned against the same thing: "If you are afraid of men and a slave to their opinions," he said, "go do something else. Go and make shoes to fit them. Go even and paint pictures which you know are bad, but which suit their bad taste. But do not keep on all your life preaching sermons which shall say not what God sent you to declare, but what they hired you to say. Be courageous."

In the epilogue to his book, *Whatever Happened to Sin?*, Carl Menninger addressed young seminarians, "Preach! Tell it like it is. Say it from the pulpit. Cry it from the housetops. What shall we cry? Cry comfort, cry repentance, cry hope. Because recognition of our part in the world's transgression is the only remaining hope."

That kind of prophetic ministry will come only when

the pastorate is a calling, not just a career.

A few years ago Georgetown University won the NCAA basketball championship. With everyone of their starters returning the next year, it appeared as though they were on the verge of a dynasty.

Immediately following the championship game there was talk of a repeat next year. When the newscasters asked coach John Thompson about it, he said, "I think our chances are terrible. It's the hardest thing in the world to come back. These kids will be cocky. Chances will be very hard. I don't expect you to believe that, but I have got to coach through."

Then coach Thompson was asked about his starting line-up next year. He said, "I put little emphasis on who starts. What's most important is who finishes."

That's what's important to the Lord also. He wants us to finish well. That's why we must watch the pitfalls.

Chapter 8

If I Had the Pastorate to Do Over Again

For years I have asked older pastors what they would do differently if they had their ministry to do over again. I asked that question of Dr. W. A. Criswell, who pastored First Baptist Church of Dallas, Texas, for 50 years. He answered, "I would preach the Bible. I would begin with the first verse of the first chapter of Genesis. If I could not find a sermon in the first verse, I would preach the whole chapter. If I couldn't find a sermon in the whole chapter, I would preach the whole book. I would preach the Bible book by book, chapter by chapter, verse by verse, word by word."

Then he added, "On Sunday nights I would preach about our Lord. I would preach through Matthew, then Mark, then Luke, then John. And when I was finished, I would start all over again."

I asked the same question of the late Ramsey Pollard, who pastored Bellevue Baptist Church, Memphis, Tennessee. He answered, "I would do four things differently. I would finish my education (he never finished college or attended seminary). I would develop more patience with my staff and with others. I would honor the person and power of the Holy Spirit more. And I would become a better man personally."

And I asked Melvin Fields, a retired minister who spent most of his years in smaller churches, what he'd do. He said, "I would prepare myself more diligently."

In more recent years, as I have grown older, young pastors are asking me that question. The question is, of course, a question of priorities. As we near the end, as we reflect on the past, our priorities become clearer.

If I had my ministry to do over again I would not write more books; I would not try to build more buildings; I would not take more revival meetings; I would not get more involved in my community. I am fairly well pleased with all those things. But there are some things I definitely would do differently. Let me share them with you.

- I would pray more.
- I would spend more time with my family.
- I would give more time to developing lay people.
- I would be more involved in my denomination.
- I would take more time off.
- I would be a better friend to my fellow pastors.

The Source of Power

If I had my ministry to do over, one thing I'd do is pray more. I never felt like my prayer life was adequate. I have read of the great saints of other generations who spent an hour or more in prayer every day. That used to bother me until I realized they lived and ministered before the telephone and the automobile and the pressures of the modern pastorate. I don't think I could have ever found that much time for prayer, but, nonetheless, I wish I had prayed more.

To neglect prayer is to neglect the source of the greatest power in our lives. If we depend on education, we get what education can do. If we depend on organization, we get what organization can do. If we depend on money, we get what money can do. If we depend on promotion, we get what promotion can do. But if we depend on prayer, we get what God can do.

I'm convinced that prayer is the principle work of a minister, and it is by it that he carries on the rest. Prayer does not fit us for greater works; prayer is the greater work.

Dr. Ralph Herring pastored the First Baptist Church, Winston-Salem, North Carolina, for years. Later, he became director of seminary extension for Southern Baptists. Before he concluded his pastoral ministry he attended an organ recital where the organ had been built by one of his kinfolk. He was impressed because the organ had 8,672 pipes. That's a fair-sized instrument. He said as he sat there looking at all those pipes, all he could think of was, "My kin built that!"

Then, he said, it was as if God spoke to him and said, "Ralph, 8,672 pipes. That's real impressive. But I want to remind you that there would not be one note from any of those pipes without the breath in the bellows."

Just so, without prayer and without the breath of the Holy Spirit upon it, we will have no great ministry.

They Are the Lord's Work

Second, if I had my ministry to do over, I'd spend more time with my family. A lot of preachers have felt this way. B. H. Carroll, longtime pastor of First Baptist Church, Waco, Texas, and founder of Southwestern Baptist Theological Seminary, was one. While his son, Guy, lay near death in Carroll's Fort Worth home, Carroll often paced in front of his house, muttering to himself, "I've taken care of the Lord's house, but not my own."

Billy Sunday, the great evangelist, had the same regrets. All four of his children died before reaching their fortieth birthdays. And, from all outward appearances, only one daughter was a Christian. Their three sons were all killed in violent accidents. Billy Sunday said, "It's funny; in the last 20 years I guess I've spoken to more than 85 million people and had the joy of seeing hundreds of thousands come to Christ . . . yet my own children, the people closest to me, have found no peace and no happiness anywhere."

Peter Lynch, who made millions a year in annual fees managing the $2 billion Magellan mutual fund, quit his job in his prime, saying, "When you start to confuse Freddie Mae, Sallie Mae, and Fannie Mae with members of your family, and remember 2,000 stock symbols but forget your children's birthdays, there's a good chance you've become too wrapped up in your work."

"You start to recognize that you're only going to exist for a little while, whereas you're going to be dead for a long time. You start wishing you'd seen more school plays and ski meets and afternoon soccer games. You remind yourself that nobody, on his deathbed, ever said: 'I wish I'd spent more time at the office.'"

I heard a minister say, "My greatest mistake in life was believing I had to complete my seminary degree at a precise time, despite the fact we had one baby when I started and a 'surprise' baby the next year. God didn't call me to neglect two babies; my ego was the voice I heard." Children are grown and gone before you know it. If you still have children at home, take the time to play with them, pray with them, and listen to them.

Apparently many ministers are neglecting not only their children, but also their wives. At any one time the legal department of the Annuity Board is dealing with more than 100 divorce cases, many of them involving ministers.

A young pastor asked an older minister, "Which is more important, my family or the Lord's work?"

The wise old man said, "My son, your family is the Lord's work." If I had it to do over, I'd remember that.

The Only Thing That Lasts

A third thing I'd do if I had my ministry to do over is to spend more time developing lay people. Floyd Bradley, in his last sermon to his congregation before retirement, said to them, "If I had my ministry to do over I'd plant more acorns and less pumpkins." I would also.

Sam Cannata, one of our Southern Baptist missionaries, said when he left Ethiopia in 1977 the Lord asked him a tough question: "What did you leave there that was eternal?" Sam said, as he reflected on his work, he realized that he had been scattering seed, not planting seed.

Then he added, "As I look back on my missionary service, the only triumphs are the lives of people I discipled."

That's the only lasting good you and I will do also. Daniel Webster wrote:

> *If we work upon marble*
> *It will perish;*
> *If we rear temples, they*
> *Will crumble into dust;*
> *But if we work upon*
> *Immortal souls*
> *We engrave on those*
> *Tablets*
> *Some things which will*
> *Brighten all eternity.*

Most of us will not be very long remembered after we are gone. If you want to make an investment in the things that will not perish, invest in developing human character.

We Baptists today are many, but we're not much. We are counting members when we ought to be weighing them. We've got to stop measuring churches by ordinary statistics: buildings and budgets and baptisms and broadcasts. We need to measure them by behavior. If we ever go as deep as we are wide, we'll be something to behold.

Working on immortal souls, making disciples, is not quick, easy work. It involves the investment of your life in the life of another person. It requires sacrifice, self-discipline, patience, and time. But it's worth it. It's the only thing that lasts.

If I had it to do over, I'd be more careful not to use people to build the work, but use the work to build people.

A World View

Another thing I would do if I had my ministry to do over is to work more in my denomination. When I started out in the ministry I would have made a great independent preacher. I didn't grow up in a Christian home or attending church. It was not until my early teen years that I became a Christian and became involved in the work of the Lord. So I had little or no background in our denomination.

In my first pastorate I was content just to work my own patch. I did not have a vision of a statewide, nationwide, or worldwide ministry. But, through the years, as I attended our state conventions and evangelism conferences, my vision was broadened and I realized that I was responsible for the whole world. I owe that broadened view of the world to my denomination. That is one of its great gifts to me.

Because of their love of freedom and fear of ecclesiastical control, Baptists have always been suspicious of organizing beyond the local church. The earliest organizational unit of Baptist life was the local association. That's where I would begin my work and then, in an ever-broadening circle, serve wherever I could in my denomination.

After graduation from seminary I began attending my local associational meetings. There I found encouragement, inspiration, and fellowship that helped me in the ministry. Grady Metcalf, pastor of First Baptist Church, Temple, Texas, and Charles Tope, pastor of First Baptist Church, Belton, Texas, were older, more experienced men who took me under their wings. They encouraged me and counseled me and helped me in my work. I owe much to those early relationships. And I could have gotten even more out of my local association if I'd just put more into it.

Someone has said, "Links together make a chain, trees together make a forest, shingles together make a roof, drops of water together make an ocean, soldiers together make an army, and churches and preachers together can make a mighty force for God, a great missionary people."

It is as simple as this, we can do more together than we can do separately. We need to be unified in God's work. We need to cooperate together. And, if I had another chance, I'd do it more.

The Devil Doesn't Take Vacations

A fifth thing I would do if I had my ministry to do over again is take more time off. I've never been very good at taking time off. Spurgeon once said, "Doing nothing is hard work for me." It was for me, too. As a result, I have worked hard to a fault. I never took a regular day off. I didn't take my full two weeks vacation more than five or six times in 35 years. That wasn't fair to me or my family. And, if I had my ministry to do over again, it's one of the things I'd change.

Early in my ministry at Green Acres, I had planned a week's vacation well in advance. Then the father of one of our young women called wanting to schedule his daughter's wedding during the time I was to be away. When my secretary told him I would be on vacation that weekend he said angrily, "Why does the preacher need a vacation? The devil never takes a vacation."

When she relayed the message to me, my response was, "I didn't know I was supposed to take the devil as my example. And if I didn't take a vacation, I'd be as mean as he is."

Years ago the late Dr. Warren Huyck, longtime pastor of First Baptist Church, West Palm Beach, Florida, said to me, "Paul, take vacations often." It was wise advice but I didn't follow it. I wish I had. I hear some preachers say, "I would rather burn out than rust out." My response today is, Why do either? Why not live out your ministry in joy and fruitfulness, and you will take better care of yourself physically.

The Lord gave us a body through which we serve him. It is not only essential, it is irreplaceable. We must take care of it. Mickey Mantle received a liver transplant June 8, 1995, at Baylor University Medical Center, Dallas, Texas, only to die of metastatic cancer on August 13 at age 63. The Hall of Fame outfielder who hit 536 career home runs in 18 seasons for the New York Yankees, was actually over the hill at 32 or 33. But, according to his own testimony, he literally wasted his life through drinking and partying.

Mantle's father died at 39 of Hodgkin's disease, cancer of the lymphatic system. The same disease also killed his grandfather and two of his brothers before they were 40. So Mantle didn't expect to live to age 50. After his transplant he said, "If I'd known I was going to live this long, I would have taken better care of myself."

None of us really knows how long we shall live, so we ought to take good care of ourselves so we can serve the Lord as long and effectively as possible.

Jesus was one of the busiest men who ever lived. There were times when the crowds pressed on him almost unmercifully. In those times when he was most busy, he often said to his disciples, "Come ye apart and rest awhile." It really comes down to this, we must either come apart or we will fly to pieces. The stress of the ministry is such that we need to take adequate time off.

This should not be a cover-up for laziness. It is simply a recognition of a basic need and how God made us.

Throwing Ropes, Not Rocks

Finally, if I had my ministry to do over again, I would be a better friend to my fellow pastors — my brother ministers. I asked Ramsey Pollard, in the visit mentioned previously, what advice he had for a young preacher. He said, "Make all the pastor friends you can. Not for the wrong reasons, but be a friend to your brothers. They will help you later on."

Life has a way of taking some strange twists. We are so intertwined that we keep bumping into one another all along life's journey. And we need one another more than we ever imagine. So we ought to make as many friends as we can along the way. We especially need to show grace and acceptance to one another.

Two of the most famous Christian preachers were contemporaries during the nineteenth century. D. L. Moody was a great American evangelist and pastor. Charles H. Spurgeon literally took Great Britain by storm through his powerful preaching of the gospel.

D. L. Moody went to London to meet Spurgeon, whom he had admired from a distance and considered to be his professional mentor. However, when Spurgeon answered the door with a cigar in his mouth, Moody fell down the stairs in shock. "How could you, a man of God, smoke that?" protested the great American evangelist.

Spurgeon took the stogie out of his mouth and walked down the steps to where Moody was still standing in bewilderment. Putting his finger on Moody's rather rotund stomach, he smiled and said, "The same way you, a man of God, could be that fat!"

We all have faults and weaknesses. They may be different from our brother, but they are no less real. Couldn't we be a little kinder to one another? Most of us are far too critical and judgmental of one another. We are not only quick to believe the worst about one another, we are anxious to.

To the Christians in Galatia, Paul wrote, "For all the law is fulfilled in one word, even this: Thou shalt love thy neighbor as thyself." Then he adds this word of warning, "But if you bite and devour one another take heed that ye be not consumed one of another" (Gal. 5:15). Biting and devouring one another — that's Christian cannibalism. We and our fellow ministers can survive persecution and poverty and even perversion. But we can't survive Christian cannibalism.

In my book, *Special Sermons for Special Days*, I tell that when I was a pastor I used to close the services on Sunday evening by inviting the children to the front to visit with me. I'd sit on the steps of the platform and as they gathered around me I would interview those who had had a birthday the previous week. I would ask them their age, their birthday, what present they liked best, and then I'd ask them to share a verse of scripture with the congregation.

One Sunday night I called the children forward and asked who had had a birthday that week. One little girl lifted her hand and I called her forward for an interview.

When I asked her birthday, I discovered she had not had a birthday that week. Her birthday was still months away. So I asked her why she had come forward. She said, "I'm standing up for my brother."

She then told me her little brother had his birthday that week, but he was too timid to come forward and be interviewed. And she didn't want his birthday to come and go without notice. So she was standing up for her brother.

It occurs to me that if ever there was a time when we ought to stand up for our brother, it's now. If ever there was a place where we ought to stand up for our brother, it is the church.

A woman, in a letter to the editor of *Christianity Today,* indicted many of us when she reprimanded some Christian leaders for being critical of other leaders. She said, "If you can't support your Christian brothers, at least don't side with their tormentors."

Our job as Christian leaders is not to throw rocks, but to throw ropes. We need to spend more time edifying one another and less time classifying one another. We are here to see one another through, not to see through one another. I've tried to do that to my fellow ministers through the years, but I would do more of it if I had a second chance.

I have spent this chapter telling you what I would do if I had my ministry to do over again. The fact is, my ministry is not over yet. The church called me to be a pastor. The Lord called me into the ministry. I gave up the pastorate to come to the Annuity Board. I will give up the ministry when he calls me home. So I have recommitted myself to better doing these six things. I ask you to join me in this renewal. Do it for your own sake. Do it for the sake of God's kingdom.

Chapter 9

Watch the Little Things

In July, 1995, the scheduled launch of our U.S. space shuttle was scratched at the last minute. The reason? Woodpeckers had damaged the exterior of the ship and made it unsafe for flying.

How much do we spend on one space shuttle? Ten, twenty million dollars? And yet woodpeckers grounded the thing. It was a simple reminder of the power of little things. It is often so in life — little things exert great power. Even the scriptures speak of little foxes that spoil the vines (Song of Sol. 2:15).

A. J. Gordon reminds us that the day of small things can become the life of biggest and best things. A small word spoken at the right time may set a whole life straight. A gentle smile may brighten the way for a person with a heavy load. A small bit of time with the book and the knee bent will hallow the day's tasks. The still, small voice listened to may turn the world's tide. The small hand in God's hand becomes big.

The opposite is also true. It is not the mountain that

wears us out — it is the grain of sand in our shoe. It is most often the little things that cause the biggest headaches. I want to close this book on shepherding the sheep in smaller churches by reminding you of some little things that can play big parts in determining your success or failure. As Oliver Wendell Holmes reminds us, if we do the little things, the big things will take care of themselves.

Dress for Success

One thing that can affect your effectiveness is the way you dress. *Forbes* Magazine said, "Dress like a bum and you act like a bum. Dress like a gentleman and you act like a gentleman. Clothes create an image you must live up to."

It is not necessary to have a large and expensive wardrobe to dress well. Three or four suits are sufficient. Just make sure they are always cleaned and pressed, that your tie and socks are coordinated, and that your shoes are polished, even the soles.

My advice is, "Dress for success." That's one of the best ways to achieve it.

Watch Your Weight

A second little thing that can affect your effectiveness is your physical well-being. You should watch your weight and keep yourself well groomed. Some people have genetic problems that make it difficult to control their weight, but for most of us a good diet and regular exercise program will do the trick. These things not only keep you physically fit and mentally alert, but they set a good example for your people.

I once had an evangelist in my church who must have

been at least 100 pounds overweight. When the revival was over, one of our ladies said to me, "Pastor, thank you for setting the right example for us in staying physically fit." Until that comment, I guess I hadn't realized that everything we do is a witness to our people.

I simply remind you that the body is the baggage you must carry through life. The more excess baggage, the shorter the trip. So be a weight watcher.

Pulpit Manner

Recently, New Mexico Representative Bill Richardson faced off with Iraq's leader Saddam Hussein in an effort to free two Americans imprisoned on charges of illegally crossing into Iraq. The New Mexican congressman followed protocol and brought a gift of an American Indian pot to Mr. Hussein. But his efforts almost collapsed when he blundered by crossing his legs and revealing the bottom of his shoe.

The pistol-wearing president promptly walked out, leaving an interpreter to explain that showing the sole of one's shoe is an insult in Arabic culture.

Showing the bottom of your shoes is not quite that serious in church, but when I was a student at Southwestern Seminary years ago, my preaching professor told us when we sat on the platform not to cross our legs, but to always sit with our feet flat on the floor. That may have been a personal bias of his, but it stuck with me. It does look better. And, when you are standing behind the pulpit, keep your coat buttoned.

The way you conduct yourself in the pulpit is another thing that will affect your effectiveness. These are little things, but they do matter.

An Attitude of Gratitude

Another little thing that can affect your effectiveness is an attitude of gratitude. When people do things for you, no matter how small, thank them. Keep a good supply of "thank you" notes close at hand and use them regularly. It takes just a minute to express your appreciation for a kindness and it will leave a lasting impression.

I began this practice years ago and have never abandoned it. It has become such a part of my life that occasionally people who do something for me will say, "Now, preacher, you don't need to write and thank me for this." But, I do anyway. I am determined that gratitude will not die in me. And, the only way to keep gratitude alive is by expression.

Forrest Gump said, "Always say 'thank you,' even if you don't mean it." Do say thank you. And, do try to mean it. If you will do this, one day you'll thank me for encouraging you to fulfill this simple courtesy.

A Cluttered Desk and a Cluttered Mind

All of my life I have heard it said, "A cluttered desk is the sign of a cluttered mind." I can't substantiate that, but I do know a neat desk presents a good image.

But how do you keep your desk clean with so much to do? For one thing, mail should be answered promptly. I learned a long time ago it is best to handle a piece of mail only once. So, when a letter arrives, if possible I answer it immediately. The subject matter is already on my mind, and if I answer the letter immediately I can dismiss the subject and discard the paper. It is the same with returning phone calls. It is better if you don't let them accumulate. And, if material needs to be filed, do it at once. These things don't guarantee success, but they sure make you look like a success.

Walk and Talk Naturally

All of my life I have had people say to me, "You sure don't look like a preacher." I've always wondered, what is a minister supposed to look like?

I feel like Walker Johnson. Someone asked him, "If a person saw you walking down the street would they be able to recognize you as a minister?" He replied, "I hope not. But, I hope they wouldn't be surprised if they found out."

Strive always to be natural in your manner and unaffected in your speech. In those ways, try to be like everyone else.

You've Gotta Have Class

The Bible says, "Whatsoever you do, do it heartily as to the Lord" (Col. 3:23). That means, at least in part, that everything we do should be done with class. And class is one of those little things that can affect your effectiveness.

By class I mean a thing should be done properly, in good taste, with dignity, in a way that you and your people can be proud of. There is no place for shoddiness in God's work. After all, we represent the King.

I was in a revival meeting in a small church several years ago. During the first service of the revival the pastor stood to introduce me. He said, "Paul has a wife named Mary (my wife's name is Cathy). He was in his former church for 10 years I believe." He then turned to me and asked, "Isn't that right?" I replied, "Seventeen years."

He then said, "He's been at the Annuity Board for two years, I believe." Again, he turned to me and asked, "Isn't that right?" I replied, "Three and a half years." At that point, trying to make a joke out of a bungled situation, I stood up, extended my hand, and introduced myself to him. All the while he had my resumé in his hand. But, he hadn't taken time to read it so he could make a proper introduction.

In a few minutes the minister of music stood to sing a solo. He thanked the organist, the pianist, and the choir for their support. Then he turned to the congregation and said, "And I thank you for putting up with me."

There are a lot of churches that ought to be thanked for the things they put up with from us.

Preserve Your Work

While serving in a smaller church you have a great opportunity to build a sermon reservoir for the future. If you preach solid, biblical sermons, if you do good exegesis, and if you use good illustrations, your sermon will never be out of date. So, manuscript your sermons and save them for the future. Good sermons are seldom born fully grown. Most of them develop and mature over time. If you save them, new material can be added as you find it.

I was once in a revival meeting with a pastor who later taught at one of our Baptist schools. He asked me how I preserved my sermons. When I explained that I manuscripted every sermon (usually after I have preached it) he said, "You will make it. You will succeed."

As I look back across the years, I am convinced that doing good work and preserving the results has aided me throughout my ministry.

Be a Good Investor

Another thing that will help you to be successful is to learn to invest wisely. George Burns once quipped, "People tell me I should save for a rainy day. With my luck, it will never rain, and I will be stuck with all that money."

It rains on all of us eventually, and having something saved when it does will help. For the average working person to get ahead in life he must save at least 10 percent of his money and invest it wisely. He must not only work himself, he must put his money to work. He must get to the place where his money makes money for him if he is ever to get ahead.

The best thing you can do to accomplish this is put your money in the hands of a professional money manager, invest it in the stock market, and leave it there. A study for Towneley Capital Management Inc. found that one dollar invested in 1963 would have grown to $24.30 by 1993 if the investor had stayed in the stock market the entire time and put dividends back into the stocks.

Consider another eye-opening example. Suppose you had the foresight and discipline to put away $1,000 a year from ages 20 to 29, and then stopped, without adding another penny; by age 60 your retirement nest egg (assuming a nine percent return) would have grown to a solid $219,717. But had you waited instead until age 30 to begin investing that same $1,000 and kept doing so for the next 30 years, you would have amassed only $148,575.

Because of your procrastination, you would have had to put up three times as much to reap about a third less.

That's where the Annuity Board of the Southern Baptist Convention can help you. We retain the most professional money management possible and we offer it at truly competitive expense. Because of our size, even modest accounts get top level management. Funds placed with us can be tax-deferred, the state convention often adds matching funds, and a part, or maybe all, your monthly retirement benefit can be drawn out tax-free for housing expenses in retirement if you are an ordained minister. I don't believe there is another investment opportunity for ministers equal to that of the Annuity Board.

Let me suggest five keys to building an adequate retirement income:

- Start early. If you start when you are young, you have more years in the Church Annuity Plan to accumulate money. This means more money in your account when you retire. And that means a larger benefit for you.

- Contribute adequately. Even if you start early, contributing very small amounts will not build a large account. Experts suggest you contribute 10 to 15 percent of your cash salary plus housing, within IRS limits. If you can't start there, start where you can and gradually work toward that goal. Contact the Annuity Board for a free calculation of IRS contribution limits, especially if your pay includes minister's housing allowance. With the Church Annuity Plan, both you and your church can contribute to your retirement account. And you may be eligible for additional matching contributions from your state convention. Remember, the more money that goes into the account, the larger your benefit during retirement.

- Contribute monthly. Regular monthly contributions are essential. If contributions are inconsistent, your account will be smaller and your benefit less. When called to a new church, be sure no monthly contributions are missed. Failing to participate for months or years can really reduce the benefits you receive from the Church Annuity Plan. So, contribute regularly. Contribute every month.

- Invest wisely. Compared to simply saving, investing offers the opportunity for your money to really grow. The Annuity Board has a strong investment program for the Church Annuity Plan. You may choose one or more investment funds. Earnings added to contributions are a major factor in building a large account and a better retirement benefit.

- Tax shelter. Money contributed by your church is tax deferred. Your own contributions can be tax sheltered through a written salary reduction agreement. Investment earnings are also tax deferred. Ordained ministers do not pay self-employment tax on contributions. All these advantages help your account grow faster.

The scriptures teach us that, as a shepherd of sheep, you have a spiritual duty to provide for the material needs of your family (1 Tim. 5:8). The Annuity Board exists to help individuals and churches fulfill their spiritual responsibilities by providing life, medical and disability insurance and a retirement program. So call us at 1-800-262-0511. We'll leave the light on for you.

An insurance commercial says, "The one thing worse than dying young is to outlive your money." Thousands of ministers do that out of neglect. Don't be one of them. Mark it down somewhere: It will rain one of these days. If you don't believe me, check with Noah.

Giving Your Best

Always give your best to what you do. When Jean Owen met and confessed to Willa Cather her desire to become an author, Miss Cather offered this advice: ". . . there will be times in your writing career when you are tempted to 'save' something for the great novel or story you intend to write someday. Be a spendthrift with your effort, your ideas, with the best you have in you, every single time you sit down to your typewriter."

That's good advice for the preacher also. Members of congregations who come to church regularly are entitled to the best their preacher has every time he speaks. This does not minimize other demands that are made on his time nor does it ignore an extra-heavy schedule of funerals during a particular week. But if the preacher would develop the habit of giving his best to each effort, the best would come habitually.

Someone asked Joe DiMaggio why he always played so hard. He responded, "That may be the first time some person ever came to see me play."

We never know when it will be the first time or perhaps the last time someone will hear the word of God from us. So always give your best.

Remember Who You Work For

Finally, remember who you work for. In his book, *The Longest Day*, Cornelius Ryan relates the experiences of many American soldiers involved in the D-day invasion of Europe. He tells that by war's end Ranger Bill Petty had fought from the top of Pointe du Hoc, across France and through Germany. He earned two Silver Stars, but he gave both away. "I didn't fight for medals," he said.

When the days are long, when your critics are loud, when the pay is low, when the work is laborious, remember who you work for. You're not working for medals. You work for the Lord. If one day you hear him say, "Well done, thou good and faithful servant" (Matt. 25:21), it will be reward enough.